SISTER STORIES

SISTER STORIES

It's Your Turn

STEFANIE HORNBY
& KYMN GOLDSTEIN

21
STORY
STREET

Contents

FOREWARD 2

INTRODUCTION 4

STORY KEY 7

IN A PICKLE 8

STRAWBERRIES 14

OFFICE POLITICS 18

COLLECTION 24

IN BE-TWEEN 29

OPEN 24 HOURS 32

INVISIBLE 37

LONELINESS 41

BLUE 45

SUMMER SESSIONS 53

COOKIES & DREAMS 56

COOKIEGATE 58

THE WONDER OF IT ALL 61

THE FIDGET SPINSTER 66

LATCHKEY TRAVELER 71

SOMETHING BETTER BEGINNING 78

APPENDIX I: ASSIGNMENTS FROM GINNY 85

APPENDIX II: THE THREE C'S 88

APPENDIX III: PUSS IN: BOOTY CALL 90

First Printing, 2020

FOR DELILAH

&

CLEMENTINE

FOREWARD

I wish I was writing this under different circumstances. But, as happens in life, as in writing, the story does not always end where we think it will.

We wrote these stories without purpose. Sheer determination to activate our creativity. Get our imaginative juices flowing. One story we adapted into a short play. Another we submitted to a short story contest. Then we wrote a full-length play. When we began to write, we didn't know these stories would be a catalyst to create more. The other unknown was that our five years of writing together would be all there would be.

When people say, "I'm sorry you lost your sister" or "sorry to hear she passed", I simply say "thank you" instead of "I didn't lose her. She died." Stefanie, who loved to banter about word choices, would have supported my thinking. She would have also thought there were many more stories to write about all of this.

My dear friend Scotty said, "Words have the power to create eternity". This is the first of what I hope will be many attempts to immortalize Stefanie through her own words. As she was preparing to leave this planet, one of the things she said - seemingly to nobody in particular - was "Write it! Write it!".

So from Stefanie to all of us, WRITE IT!

Kymn and Stefanie 2015

INTRODUCTION

A Note from Kymn

Envy is as good of a place as any to start. Sunday night 2015, FUN HOME wins Best Musical of the Year at the Tony's and I'm envious. The kind of envy only a writer who isn't writing feels. I don't suffer from writer's block or lack of inspiration. I suffer from not putting pen to paper. Plenty of good ideas never finished. I'm consistent at least in that way.

Around this time, my sister Stefanie sent me a text. She was busy raising two girls, Clementine and Delilah, and was herself in a creative wasteland. We would have been satisfied simply commiserating, but Ginny, my brilliant and too-often-ignored spouse, hatched a plan. "I'm going to give you two a writing assignment."

We embarked on a journey together. Both starting a story, writing half, then sending it to the other to finish. Instead of hard work, it felt fun. Opening each other's word document to discover what the other person had written was like receiving a gift. A prize. As we went on, the stories got finished. Then we took one and adapted it into a short play. Then we wrote a longer play together. At the same time, real life happened – exciting, mundane, hard, shocking. Through it all we kept writing.

I learned a lot about writing – and life – through this process. The things that seem insurmountable in one moment, aren't really that important in the bigger scheme of things. I also learned that it doesn't really matter what you write, or what happens with it.

Happiness happens in the act of writing. Sharing it with someone, is an act of love.

A Note from Stefanie

On my end, I had been a very (though not well-compensated) busy local actress in the San Francisco/Bay Area prior to the birth of my first daughter in 2010. It was creatively rewarding, and I loved it. I did theater and indie films... until my daughter and her sister, three years later, took up most of my spare time. (And they didn't even want me to do "voices" when I read their story books, something I felt kinda bad about, until I heard Robin Williams say the same thing about *his* daughter. (And *he* could do characters!)

I then started to do paid acting gigs — mostly corporate video shoots, which were less of a time-suck and satisfied me to a degree, but lacked the creative fulfillment of my previous acting work. I had written a couple of one-woman shows, and a few sketches, so when Kymn suggested working on a play together, I jumped at the idea.

I think around the same time, my twin sis, Stacy, came up with another writing project for us, which Kymn and I both adored and followed up on. Unfortunately, my twin didn't have the time to squeeze in a regular writing assignment, as it were, so Kymn and I took Ginny's advice and started doing our own, with her idea for prompts. We continued working on the play we began, but these assignments were a more relaxed, low-pressure way to "work out", create, without too much focus on the outcome.

It ended up being very fulfilling and exhilarating to finish, then be allowed to read the other's story. It was important to have someone to whom to be accountable, as well. (That Ginny's a taskmaster!) Because, frankly, Facebook and web news sites were too easy to devote time to. With nothing to show for that lost time, either. I go back and read our finished assignments, our stories, and I think, "Wow. I don't even remember writing that. Where did that come from?" And it's fascinating to see another mind take a completely different route with your story or idea for a story.

This has been a very liberating, productive and eye-opening experience. I encourage others to explore and play in a similar way, results be damned.

STORY KEY

The stories presented here are in their original, unedited form.

♡ Stefanie
♡♡ Kymn

IN A PICKLE

♡

"You must really like pickles," she said, the first time I showed her my house.

As with my life, I'd let her into my closet too early. I was already feeling pangs of regret. And panic.

"No. Not at all. Actually, I can't stand them. Except when they come in little wooden bowls at Canter's Deli as a harbinger of great things to come."

She'd been referring to my collection of pickle jars. I had ushered her into my bedroom, pushed aside my wrinkled pile of dry clean-only clothes (which were really my wear-one-too-many-times-and-then-never-again clothes) and shown her my secret.

Twenty-nine Vlasic pickle jars filled to the brim with coins. I held the thirtieth in my hand. It was two-thirds full. I explained that once it reached capacity, I was leaving my husband Todd.

First, I explained the significance of the vessels to my new friend:

"My grandmother used to mix frozen orange juice concentrate with water and store the concoction -- hell, let's call it 'orange juice' -- in pickle jars. I don't know why she did that. Then she'd pour it into a cheap, tan, plastic pitcher she kept in her kitchen to serve it from. I can 'pitcher the pitcher' -- tee hee."

My new friend laughed.

"I think it drove my grandfather crazy. 'Libby, I don't want to drink pickle-flavored OJ. You want a glass pitcher? I'll buy you a glass pitcher.' But he accepted it, as *she* did many of *his* foibles. They lasted together 52 years, and frankly, I cannot imagine. So, I'm using pickle jars so that I can be very sure I want to do it. Like, "Can't you just deal with what bugs you about him? Bubbie did it. Grandpa did it.'"

"And what bugs you about him? What's so bad that you're saving coins in clandestine pickle jars, 'til you have the money to leave?"

"He leaves coins all over the house."

And now all he had to do was drop a week's worth of coins, and I was a free woman.

Ours was a fast-tracked friendship, mine and Stella's. We'd met at a one-day career conference, ate lunch at the same table, and divulged info about ourselves we'd never told anyone before. She'd let me in on her kleptomania past; I'd confessed I'd never smoked pot but let my friends (and husband) assume I had. There's something refreshing about someone who wears her heart on her sleeve, but then you end up sharing too much, as well, and feeling vulnerable. That's what happened. Was it because we were both neurotic and gregarious Jews with a lack of neurotic and gregarious Jews in our lives? Or some other -- greater -- lack?

We'd commiserate about our childless marriages, unfulfilled dreams, and seemingly dead-end jobs. We'd claimed to have carried Purell before anyone else. We'd laughed over the liberating feeling of learning to throw away the tiny remnants of a bar of soap and breaking open a new one with guilt-free gusto. We connected in a way I didn't know platonic adults could. It was like Jessie DeLorenzo and I in 6th grade discussing KISS over peanut butter sandwiches and slushy, frozen-the-night-before Welch's grape juice in a can.

I was attracted to her openness and her fiery eyes.

So, when I showed her the pickle jars and saw the nonplussed look on her face -- a look that said my new soul mate didn't seem to get it -- I quickly spun into damage-control mode. I wanted to un-show her. Our relationship seemed to be veering off-course, as if it were over before it had even begun. It was as if our unsatisfying lives were on unequal playing fields now.

I couldn't merely laugh it off: "Ha ha. Just kidding! I'm just too lazy to roll them and too cheap to take them to CoinStar."

So I lied. And not just a little white lie, either.

"We had a son. Euripides. Four years ago he choked and died on a nickel Todd left lying on the laundry room floor. I'm not sure I can ever forgive him." With that, tears rolled down my cheeks and I sobbed effortlessly, almost as if I were mourning the impending loss of my new Before-Anyone-Else Friend.

Later that night, gripped by fear for having told such an amazing and horrific lie, I wept. The next morning, I awoke expecting those tears, the real ones, to have washed away my sins. I went about my day as I would have before the *closet-pickle-jar-choking-son* incident occurred. Before Todd's time started to run out, and poor imaginary Euripides had died. And before my new friend Stella held me in her warm empathetic embrace. I didn't realize I had opened a door that could not easily be re-shut. Onto a series of events I would watch unfold with a combination of reckless awe and stone cold horror.

"I signed us up for grief class," Stella said. We were at the corner café down the street sharing an onion bagel with cream cheese. The moment before, I had felt we were back on track. The perfect match. Stella having opted for the bottom half of the bagel, "her favorite," she said, and me taking the top.

"Oh geez Louise. My goodness." I didn't know what to say. "Thank you so much, but that's too much to ask of you. You have done so much already." She told me, "It was meant to be" and proceeded to tell me a terrible story about losing her closest childhood friend to a freak tetherball accident.

That's when I should have pulled my own covers. Copped to it. Taken my medicine, so to speak, and kissed our blossoming friendship goodbye. I should have, except instead, I stood up, put my hands on her shoulders and said, "Sometimes the sadness strikes hard and knocks you off your feet, like a wave crashing in the ocean." Which might be true, except I've only been in the ocean once as a kid. My heart raced.

I left Stella and stopped at Elliot's Drug Store for lip balm and a bag of cough drops. A number of customers hovered near the cash register waiting for their prescriptions. I looked at my watch and figured I'd come back later when it was less busy. Then I heard, "Excuse me, Miss? Over here." The pharmacist waved me over and handed me a small, stapled white bag.

"Are you getting those two items too?"

I nodded.

"Great, let me ring them up for you. Have you taken this prescription before? You know not to operate heavy machinery while on it?"

"Oh yes, thanks, I have." I replied without a second thought. Then added for effect, "Strong.".

The pharmacist seemed satisfied and smiled, and I proceeded to take Mrs. Henderson's little white bag along with my lip balm and my cough drops out the front door of the store. I wondered for a moment if taking Mrs. Henderson's pills would cause her an early demise, but then realized that it was her own fault for not planning ahead and letting it go until she had only one pill left or worse – none. *What kind of a person doesn't plan ahead?*

I hurried back to my errand-running and didn't give it another thought. Until I reached the grocery store.

At Shoprite, I bought twelve Cornish game hens from the

butcher for a dinner party I wasn't having for the Stanford Alumni Club of which I was not a member. The man behind the meat counter, a sort of weekend chef himself, seemed thrilled to give me his tips and tricks for preparing them. Afterwards, I ran into Sally Simmons at the gas station and told her I couldn't stop to chat because I was en route to the airport to catch the noon flight to Chicago for my uncle's funeral. Then my boss called my cell phone, wanting to know where I was. I told him I was terribly sick. Woman stuff, ovaries. Meant to call him earlier but had just then been released from the hospital. He sounded so concerned, I felt a pang somewhere deep down inside.

I wanted to stop, really, but everything seemed out of control. In a way it was liberating to say whatever I wanted. Be whomever I wanted. *Devil may care*, I thought to myself. But that pang kept on panging. *Better head home,* I thought. *Maybe things will be normal again if I can just get home to the safety of my own four walls.*

The front door was ajar when I arrived, and I considered for a moment, *maybe he's left*. Hesitantly, I walked in, hands full of packages from my morning shopping spree. Pockets full of newly secured change.

"You're home from work early," Todd said.

Without a second thought I answered "Yes... Office Appreciation Day. We celebrate by working only half a day." Since I hadn't been to the office that day, nor did I ever appreciate being at the office, I shrugged it off to 'acting as if'.

"Hey babe, what's all this about?"

Sitting atop the dining room table were the thirty Vlasic pickle jars. Except... they were now empty.

"Wha... where," I whispered. "Where are the coins?" I felt the pang.

"They're in that pillowcase. You saving up for Armageddon? I'll take them in for you.

He beamed like the proud father Euripides never had.

"Let's keep a couple hundred and go out for a nice dinner. Wanna invite your new friend Stella? She has a husband or something?"

And again it happened.

"On, poor Stella. She's such a sick woman. I think the cancer has gone to her brain. She doesn't make much sense. I don't think we'll be seeing much of her anymore."

I was in the bathroom brushing my teeth Thursday morning, when the recycling truck came. I rinsed down one of Mrs. Henderson's pills, as the pickle jars were launched out of the trash can, sent soaring through the air, and came crashing down.

STRAWBERRIES

♡♡

They call it the Halloween house because it is always dark except for one lone, lit room that faces the street and remains illuminated day and night. The house sits on an oversized corner lot, at a busy intersection with a stop sign, in a residential neighborhood. It's a shortcut for commuters coming to and from their 9-5 jobs. The front yard is neglected. Old plants sit shriveled brown in the hot sun. The wooden window frame and front door are parched beneath faded paint, baking away day after day.

Geraldo stands straight and tall beside his metal folding chair on the corner, where the two streets meet, under his large, faded rainbow umbrella. It is ten o'clock a.m. on Tuesday. His starched buttoned down shirt and khaki pants are still fresh and unwrinkled. Erma, his wife of twenty-two years, dresses him in the morning with an outfit she has pressed and hung on hangers the night before. She believes that everything in life is a gift from God and that you show your gratitude through your daily actions, which includes how you dress. Geraldo doesn't know if he believes in God, but he believes in Erma.

Geraldo grew up on the eastside of Los Angeles with three older sisters and a younger brother. He is used to having women tell him what to do. He speaks Spanish as a second language. Erma, who originally comes from Guatemala, speaks Spanish first. Geraldo thinks it's romantic to speak Spanish with Erma. When they fight, which they rarely do, they always yell at each other in English first. His sisters all have white-collar jobs; one is an administrative assistant, one works in a bank, the eldest one works for a local television station where she puts the ads on the air. His brother is back in night school, after running in with some not so nice people, he's trying to start his life over again. His siblings don't understand him. "Why do you choose to sell fruit on a corner each day?" they often ask. Geraldo never tries to explain.

By eleven fifty-five a.m. Tuesday, he's sold two sliced mangoes, four mixed fruit salads, several coconuts with bendable straws to drink the water out with, and a flat of strawberries to a woman in a black Lexus. She gets out of her car and stands in the shade of the umbrella as they have a nice, but short, conversation about last night's hockey game after he notices a King's decal in her window. He loads the flat into her trunk and watches as she drives away realizing how hot the sun now feels bouncing off the asphalt. I've got to replace my sunglasses, he thinks to himself.

Geraldo picks up his folding chair and moves it away from the fruit display and umbrella. He places it on the small dirt hill that sits in front of the Halloween house in place of the lawn. A large Sycamore tree now provides a swatch of shade, its branches reaching over the yard. He sits down and eats a few slices of melon, and feeling a bit sleepy decides to close his eyes for a moment. Without realizing it, and for an unspecified amount of time, Geraldo dozes off.

♡

When he awakens, things have changed. His umbrella is upturned; his fruit display lies in ruins. Boxes have been ravaged; his table is missing. Rubbing his heavy eyelids, he notices coconuts and grapefruits smashed to bits in the middle of the road and watches as they get further pulverized by each passing car. He surveys the scene and sees even more destruction. His beautiful honeydew and *piel de sapo* melons seem to have been violently hurled against the side of the Halloween house. He cannot imagine a slumber so deep that the sounds of such vandalism hadn't disrupted it.

He thinks to himself, "What would Erma do?" and as the answer arrives, begins to clean up the produce remains. He improvises with a makeshift broom fashioned from a fallen Sycamore branch. He picks up a large box to gather the newly-created compost. That is when he notices the sole survivor: an unperturbed basket of strawberries, shining a stunning red in the mid-afternoon sun. Erma would call this God's little gift for the day. He smiles to himself as he realizes this and puts one to his lips.

It takes Geraldo the better part of an hour to clean up, and he discovers he is hungry and has either slept or labored through his usual lunch hour. He devours the sandwich Erma has lovingly prepared the night before and then moves on to the leftover empanadas. For dessert, he dives into Erma's decadent sweet bread soaked in syrup, with a couple of strawberry chasers. Satiated and almost recovered from the emotional blow of the day's violation, he readies himself to head home. As he does so, the morning's black Lexus pulls up in front of him.

The Kings' fan gets out and inquires after the missing fruit, assuming Geraldo has had a banner day. She has come to replenish her dwindling strawberry supply... was wishing she'd bought a second flat. He shows her his remaining basket and offers it to her. She hands him a hundred-dollar bill, tells him to keep the change. He declines but thanks her for helping to restore his faith in humanity. She waves and drives off.

As dusk approaches, Geraldo gathers his chair, umbrella and stand. His load will be lighter than usual today. He is eager to see

Erma, hear her take on the vandalism. He wonders what she will be making for dinner, what aromas will greet him as he passes the threshold of their small but charming home. He notices the sun going down and how it seems to be getting darker earlier these days. He does not notice that the light in the Halloween house has been extinguished.

OFFICE POLITICS

Humming is Lazy Singing.

Gerilyn boosts herself up out of her chair and peers over the top of her cubicle, trying to figure out who the hummer is.

"Hmm, hmm, Night Fever, Night Fe-ver... You know how to do it."

Is that what they're humming? Hard to tell without the actual words, but Gerilyn is good with music. Hard to ignore those faint hums that latch onto her mind, playing over and over again in her head for the rest of the day.

"YOU'RE HUMMING!" she yells.

It flies out of her mouth into the office air. She is shocked at first but then hopes that for once her passive-aggressiveness will pay off. However, five minutes later...

"Hmm-hmm... you got me on my knees."

LAYLA!

At least the hummer has a diverse music library to pull from. And they are actually in key. If only they were not in the office within earshot of Gerilyn's desk. She can't for the life of her figure out who it is. It started about a week ago, which could be a clue;

except for there are no new employees sitting in her section. So the melodious perpetrator is someone who's been around for a while.

Next to Gerilyn sits Carl. Father of three, mid-40's, button-down shirt untucked, jeans and inexpensive, black leather shoes. On the other side sits Courtney, 20-something, 24/7 social media maven, unnecessarily happy all the time. And from the cell phone conversations Gerilyn overhears, an avid and prolific dater. Across is Morgan – Gay guy, meticulous, slender with sideburns. Gerilyn's not a big fan of sideburns especially on such a handsome guy. They block out too much of his face.

Each day, a core group eats lunch together in the office kitchen. The crux of their conversations revolve around the New York Times crossword puzzle which they collectively do. It's Monday, the easiest day of the puzzle and the quickest one for them to finish. Fridays are the hardest, with Gerilyn and a select few others answering most of the questions. Gerilyn waits until the puzzle is finished to ask, "Has anyone noticed we have a new 'hummer' in the office?"

"No, but someone made a coffee stain on the carpet outside my cube. About the size of a baseball." Carl shares.

"Someone etched 'Fuck You' in the third stall of the ladies' room. Only they spelled it

'F-C-K You'. Idiots." Morales says. Her first name is Diana but everyone calls her Morales. She sits on the other side of Carl.

"Was it the third stall from the left or the third stall from the right?" Courtney asks.

"Nearest the door!" Jill blurts out clearly not in the mood and tired of everyone's complaining. She has to fire someone after lunch, the worst part of her job. She is the only one in their group who has an office of her own with a door.

"We're off topic" Gerilyn adds. "I need to figure out who the mystery hummer is. I can't bear another day of it".

"I haven't heard it", Courtney says.

"Me neither", Phillip chimes in.

"I think writing graffiti on a wall is way worse than humming." Morales announces. She can always be counted on to take the opposite side of any conversation. She can't understand why Gerilyn is making such a big deal about it.

"It's not a one-or-the-other kind of thing, is it?" Carl wonders aloud.

Everyone ignores him.

"It's got to be someone who wears headphones." Gerilyn says. "That's got to be a select list, right?"

"I wear headphones!" Courtney offers up.

"Which is why you don't hear the hummer." Says Gerilyn.

"I have to go get on a conference call" Jill says to nobody in particular, as she rolls her eyes and leaves.

Gerilyn looks at the clock and sighs. She dreads going back to her desk for more humming.

"You can always get your own headphones. Then you wouldn't hear it either", Courtney offers.

"You can change cubes", says Carl.

"Yeah, ask if you can move", Ramona agrees.

But Gerilyn has a coveted spot by the window that overlooks the street below. She's not going to give it up for a hummer.

Tuesday proves to be no better.

"Oh, I've been to the desert on a horse with no name, hmm hmm hmm hmm hmm hmm hmm hmm..."

This was unbearable. Who can it possibly be? Who? WHO?

"Hmm hmm hmm hmm knocking at my door? Hmm hmm hmm, don't come around here no more."

MEN AT WORK. Ironic, since this man, or woman, was so not working. MEN AT HUMMING. Or even if he is AT WORK, he/she is keeping Gerilyn from working.

Okay. It has to be someone in their 40s, or older, right? Maybe Carl. Who else would know these old songs? Courtney? Did she listen to Oldies/Classic Rock stations? Was she being "retro"? Maybe Morgan went clubbing, and they had special 70s or 80s Nights? Nah. He talked about seeing films and plays and concerts at the Bowl. How can she figure this out? And more importantly, how can she put an end to it?

It is so distracting and infuriating, she has to get out of the office for lunch. She quickly heats her frozen Trader Joe's Chicken Tikka Masala in the kitchen microwave and flees the scene. She skips Tuesday's puzzle. It's always so easy and banal, and she hates feeling superior and frustrated with her co-workers' erroneous answers – answers that ended up being red herrings and throwing off the whole puzzle.

She settles outside the building, near the patch of grass where some twenty-somethings are throwing a frisbee – "I better not get hit in the head by that damned thing" – balances her Crystal Geyser bottled water on the bench next to her and realizes she's forgotten a fork.

"God Damnit. Goddamn hummer. Can't concentrate on anything now. Mofo has got me on my knees."

Wednesday finds her one step closer – and yet further – from determining the culprit. Her prime suspect, Carl, is out of the office at a dentist appointment when the sailors were saying Brandy was a fine girl, but not in so many words. Mostly hums.

She is determined to bring it up again at the lunch table. But when she gets there, Ramona holds court for forty minutes with a soliloquy about her neighbor and fumigating with orange oil, so Gerilyn works on the puzzle almost entirely on her own and keeps quiet.

"I'm going crazy," she says on Thursday. "If I have to listen to it one more day, I might take it up with HR."

"Maybe you really are going crazy," Morales says, with a smile. "My cousin was just diagnosed with schizophrenia after complaining of hearing songs no one else did..." Her smile faded as she thought of poor Cousin Pete.

Gerilyn thinks about that for a second. Then dismisses it with a wave of her pencil, finishes the puzzle with only a smidgen of uncertainty and returns to her computer to see how blogger Rex Parker has filled in the southwest corner. Who was the author of the short story "MS. Found in a Bottle"? EAPOE? Who was Eapoe?

And then it happened: "Hmm hmm in a bot-tle. Message in a hmm hmm." She stood up. But this time, on her chair. And then, her desk.

"CAN NO ONE ELSE HEAR IT?! IT'S HIDEOUS! HIDEOUS! I'M GOING MAD! I'M GONNA MURDER SOMEONE!!!"

And then she remembers something from deep in the recesses of her memory, from high school English. She bookmarked the crossword blog and did a quick google search.

Traded Parker for Poe.

Edgar Allan Poe. E.A. Poe:

It grew louder –louder –louder! And still the men chatted pleasantly, and smiled. Was it possible they heard not? Almighty God! –no, no! They heard! –they suspected! –they knew! –they were making a mockery of my horror!-this I thought, and this I think. But anything was better than this agony! Anything was more tolerable than this derision! I could bear those hypocritical smiles no longer! I felt that I must scream or die! And now –again! –hark! Louder! Louder! Louder! Louder!

"Villains!" I shrieked, "dissemble no more! I admit the deed! –tear up the planks! Here, here! –It is the beating of his hideous heart!"

Maybe Morales is onto something? Maybe no one else heard it because it IS in her head? Can she be mad?

The next day, Friday, Jill brings in Krispy Kremes. Courtney calls in sick. And hark! The humming was no more.

COLLECTION

It was not a particularly dark or stormy night. Nevertheless, danger was a-knockin'. With both fists.

Someone was in for a wild one. Only he didn't know it yet. He went about his business, heating up his Stouffer's Mac 'n' Cheese, popping open his PBR, turning on the Bachelorette finale and expecting his usual lackluster, uneventful Monday night.

But Wimpy had pissed off one too many creditors. He never did get around to paying for those hamburgers, those promised Tuesday payments never did materialize.

Now he was in trouble.

It was during the Rose Ceremony that he heard the sound. Not a good time to be interrupted. And certainly not by one of the pesky neighbors who usually rapped on his door for a cup of flour; or with a hand-delivered piece of misdelivered mail; or to turn down the music (how can you listen to Rush adequately when you share a wall with an early-rising immigration lawyer?).

He ignored the light rapping, knowing it was obvious he was home but could maybe pass for being momentarily indisposed.

The light rapping turned to persistent knocking, which – in turn – become aggressive banging. With both fists.

"Why don't I have a goddamn peephole? I should bring this up with Phil when I drop off the rent next week. Or the week after. Or the one after that..."

Still, he figured, there must be a good reason for the urgency. Maybe Apartment 22 was on fire again, and they all needed to evacuate or something.

Opening the door ever so slightly, as if there were a "protective" chain to be able to see who was about to kick down his door, he spied someone in black-and-white stripes. And a wide-brimmed black hat. Almost comical-looking, except for the nasty look on his face. Wimpy had no choice but to let the guy enter. He knew what it was about. He had the feeling in his gut, a feeling similar to that left by a Quarter Pounder with cheese, extra mayo. (Do Quarter Pounders even have mayo? Must look that up. But he digests... er digresses...)

"Sit down, Friend", he said, to lessen the tension.

Friend stood.

"Can I offer you some tea? Coffee?"

The visitor shook his head but finally sat in a chair by the window, between the catbox and toppling piles of junk mail and past due notices. Between the litter and the letters, as it were. He picked one up. A letter, not a cat turd, although frankly, both were equally neglected by Wimpy, who usually ended up tossing them down the apartment garbage chute every two weeks.

He opened the envelope, read its contents, crumpled it up and chucked it over his shoulder. Finally, he spoke:

"You know why I've come."

It was not a question.

♡♡

"Is it about the ketchup packs?" He wasn't sure whether it was politically correct to use ketchup or catsup in this scenario.

Friend shook his head.

"The special orders?" Wimpy tried. "I know how they upset you."

Friend stood and brushed off the front of his pants, although Wimpy couldn't help notice it was more for credibility than crumbs. He turned and separated the mini blinds with his forefinger and thumb, peering out onto the street. What's he looking for, after all?

"I've got no beef with you." He finally said.

Wimpy exhaled, a little too loudly. Act natural he thought.

"Bob's dead."

The streetlight shone through the slits in the blinds and Wimpy could see tear stains on Friend's cheeks beneath the line of his black mask. He had often wondered why wear a mask anyway with such a crazy get up. It's not like anyone wouldn't recognize him. He wanted to ask Friend about it but it didn't seem the appropriate time or setting.

"But why Bob?"

"Why don't you ask yourself that?" Friend challenged him. Wimpy thought, I sort of am asking myself, but before he could articulate that, Friend continued. "Because of us. And we very well could be next."

"Wait... wait, wait, wait, wait!"

Wimpy automatically started stuttering and backing up towards the door. It was a bad habit he had developed of auto-flight even at the slightest disturbance.

"Listen, Bob was a big boy. If he got himself into trouble, well then, that's on him."

"Don't you dare go all trans-fat free on me. Did-he-call-you?" Friend gave him a hard stare.

Wimpy stared right back.

To be honest, it sounded vaguely familiar, but Wimpy didn't know if that was because he had actually remembered to check his machine and HAD received a call or because he had forgotten to check and HAD NOT received a call. He did remember seeing an illuminated number 1.

"Perhaps I should check the answering machine. In case there's a message there."

The answering machine laid atop a stack of old Sunset Magazines. The backyard BBQ issues were his favorite, and occasionally he would earmark articles on do-it-yourself brick laying and fire pit building in case he ever saved enough burger money to buy a home.

Wimpy pressed play. There was a lot of crackling followed by Bob's voice sounding shaky at best.

"We've got to bun together Wimpy – I mean band. We were on the right side with that McRib riot. 100% USDA approved. That preposterous dish should never have been on a regular menu. Seasonal only. But this other thing is bad. Hell hath no fury like a woman scorned."

And then the message cut off.

"The line went dead." Wimpy said.

"Or he did." Said Friend.

He could see that Friend was worried. But they had hardly done too much wrong. Made a few signs, wrote a few slogans. Rallied the troops so-to-speak. And what's more, they'd started to have some real success.

"If you're thinking your hands are clean, you're dead wrong. This one was all your idea." Friend said.

"Hamburgers are round – not squared!" Wimpy blurted out.

Rap-a-tap-tap. Rap-a-tap-tap. They both heard the friendly knock at the door and froze.

DO-NOT-OPEN-IT, Friend mouthed to him.

Wimpy moved towards the door – Friend towards the window.

"Who's there?" Wimpy said, a lilt in his voice.

"Maybe it's Jack!" Friend whispered.

Wimpy opened the door a crack, but nobody was there. A sudden shimmer caught the corner of his eye. Laying on the welcome mat... the King's crown. Wimpy gasped.

Friend turned back to the window and peered between the mini-blinds.

Across the street in the moonlight, he could see a pretty girl. Red-headed in pigtails wearing a blue and white gingham dress. In her left hand, she's holding a very large cleaver, dripping in blood.

IN BE-TWEEN

♡

You're getting ready for Candace Winterbottom's Bat Mitzvah. You can't seem to get your hair right. A bun? Curled? French Braid? Grrr. Why is it so hard to look good when you're twelve?

And why is someone named Candace Winterbottom having a Bat Mitzvah anyway? You're more Jewish than she is, surely. Your grandpa... whom you never met, but still... was half-Jewish. And you inherited his name. Bergstein. So there, Candace Winterbottom. Take that, with your *Baruch atah, Adonai* and your *Shma-Yisrael.*

Fake Jews. Like Fake News, only more dangerous. Because they get money and gifts and huge, extravagant parties.

But really, this is your father talking. You know nothing about this stuff. All you know is YOUR HAIR WON'T BEHAVE AND THIS ZIT ON YOUR CHIN GOT GINORMOUS AND ALEXIS BETTER NOT WEAR HER PURPLE FLORAL DRESS THAT LOOKS TOO SIMILAR TO THE ONE YOU BOUGHT SPECIFICALLY FOR THIS OCCASION.

And what if Mark shows up, and Jason, too? What happens then? Will Alexis be so freaked out about the Jason drama that she will decide not to talk to you again? Should you ignore Christina, so no one knows you like her?

Seventh Grade Politics. Like the real stuff, only more dangerous. Because you have the rest of Middle School and all of High School to deal with these people.

But at least these people relate to you, and you to them. At least most of them care enough to compliment you on your new Uggs. Not Mom and Dad. All they care about is fighting. Who can make the other feel like the lesser person. Who's the worst parent, who does the least amount of work around the house. STOP YELLING AT EACH OTHER. YOUR DAUGHTER IS ONE WALL OVER AND CAN HEAR EVERYTHING. THE HATE IS WASHING OVER HER and she cannot wait to get out of here and go to the fake Jew's fake Bat Mitzvah.

♡♡

Who's going to take you? Superficial and self-obsessed Mom or distant and delusional Dad? Either will work. You've got a plan and you've got to get going.

By the way, life is SO unfair. Last summer's vacation was a perfect example. Everyone you know went to Belize. Well, some went to Hawaii, but still. YOU SPENT 8 HOURS IN THE CAR WITH YOUR PARENTS AND ABIGAIL GOING TO NOWHERE ANYONE CARES ABOUT. Then, three days pretending to have fun with your cousins. The big "outing" was a water park. Can everyone say BORING AND LAME? Abigail loved it but she's six. Then you asked to double-pierce your ears. Mom said "no way Jose". What does that mean anyway? You cried but nobody fell for it. The best you could get was "let's revisit it when you're thirteen".

Okay, bun it is. Looking in the mirror you think, hmmm pretty good.

Candance wants her Bat Mitzvah to be NOT BORING. She's having the same DJ Bobby Newmark did. He had a photo booth and a fake tattoo station. He even had fake friends. Serious. His parents paid people to be there to get the partygoers dancing. Everyone had a blast until a couple of boys stuffed stuff down the toilets. Someone wrote with a Sharpie on the wall. Monday at school it was all anyone talked about. That's when Candace said she wanted her party to be epic too.

What if both of them are taking you? Now they're fighting in the kitchen and you can hear them all the way downstairs. They are literally together all the time. God forbid they separate for a second.

How are you going to get it into the car without them seeing you? It will definitely be harder with two of them. I mean, you can't take a backpack to a party. You should've gone downstairs and gotten in the car first. Check out the window. What's Abigail doing down there? This family is SO frustrating. Please people - get a life. Oh great, now they're looking up waving. Coming! Big smile.

Too bad the gift's all wrapped up. Do you think she'll like the bracelet? It's only 14 karat gold. Why did she have to put you in charge of this? Think, think, think. You always leave the most important thing to the last minute! You waste so much time! That's what Mom always says. YOU DON'T HAVE A BAG DUMMY PUT IT IN YOUR UNDERWEAR!

Good thinking. You may only be twelve, and you may not be the most popular girl in class, but you are one of the smartest. One Ziploc bag of weed, a lighter and a pack of strawberry rolling papers. Have to hurry. You don't want to be late to Candace Winterbottom's Fake Bat Mitzvah and Epic After-Party.

OPEN 24 HOURS

"This is a weird place for a first date", Mandy thought as she slumped down in the orange vinyl booth and looked up at the ceiling which was a kaleidoscope of bright plastic shapes and colors. This place would be cool at two in the morning, she thought. She realized she was slouching and scowling. Her drama coach always said it's less important what one says it's how one looks when they say it.

Mandy was trying to be an actress. Chloe, her best-actress-friend who shot commercials and booked small quirky plays, told her "you're not TRYING to be an actress, you ARE an actress". Mandy didn't feel like an actress. She felt like an elementary school teacher's aide. Maybe this guy will be THE ONE. Her plan B to acting was to find Mr. Right, get married and have the life of her dreams.

"Excuse me! HELLO?"

Mandy realized someone was standing by her table.

"Are you ready to order?"

Fran was a short, old woman with a mop of white hair on her head. She stood poised and ready to pounce. Pencil and pad of paper in hand.

"Oh, I'm waiting for someone." Mandy said.

"Not like that I hope." Fran said. "You're too old to be slumped in your seat like an 8-year old. Want something to gnaw on while you wait? Bagel chips? Water? Pickles?"

"I'm fine. I think I'll wait til he gets here."

"He? So we're waiting on a HE are WE?"

Mandy shrugged.

"Well now don't you think you should have something on the table so it doesn't look like you've been waiting around thinking about him?" Fran put the paper and pencil together in one hand while she leaned down holding the edge of the table in the other.

Mandy looked down to avoid Fran's intruding gaze. "I don't know. I guess so."

"You guess so? Darn right you should, young lady! You don't want to seem needy, do you?"

Mandy wanted her to leave so bad she could taste it. She needed time alone to regroup and get herself in the right frame of mind. But Fran didn't seem to be in a hurry to go.

"Well?"

Mandy wasn't sure what the question was.

"Yes, yes yes - it seems needy. There, I answered for you. I'm going to bring you water and some pickles. And maybe a cup of coffee. How about a cup of coffee? It's obvious you are going to need my help with this date" Fran left before Mandy could respond.

"How do you know it's a date?" Mandy whispered under her breath to no one at all.

Across the fluorescent restaurant, Mandy saw Jack before Jack saw Mandy. He was standing by the hostess stand, unfocused and waiting.

♡

She looked down at her flatware, not ready to catch his eye. He looked kind, she had noticed. And like he had made an effort for the date, yet without too much attention to image. She sat up in the booth. Tried to exude confidence.

"Mandy." He was standing above her table now. She liked the way he said her name. Didn't ask if it was her. Just stated it, like "I found you." Maybe he really did *find* her. Maybe he knew who she was in a deeper sense than just recognizing her.

"Yeah?"

Why couldn't she have said "Hi, Jack", the way he had said "Mandy"? In theory, being direct is so sexy.

"I'm Jack."

"Oh. Duh. Hi, Jack. I didn't recognize you, for some reason. You look different from your profile pictures." (In fact, he looked exactly like his profile pictures.)

"Really? Weird. So... you hungry?" Jack sat. Right beside her. On the same side of the booth. Dang. That's nervy. In a good way.

"Yeah. What's good here?"

"Oh. You've never been? I like all the deli sandwiches, pretty much. Corned beef on rye. Good bowl of matzo ball soup."

"Huh. Okay. That sounds good. No. This is my first time here. I never really knew it was here, in fact."

"Whoa. Really? We always come here after shows. It's open 24 hours."

"Shows? Are you in a band? What do you play?" Drums, she knew.

"Drums."

"Oh, that's right. I kinda remember that from your profile. Cool. What kind of music? What's your band's name?"

"We're sort of Steely Dan meets Eagles, but with a punk rock vibe. Name is Hey Nineteen, for obvious reasons."

Mandy chuckled. "Cool", she said, as she made a mental note to Google "Hey Nineteen", "Steely Dan" and "Eagles", since the obviousness was eluding her.

"Maybe I'll hear you sometime," she offered, feigning an air of confidence, herself.

"I'd like that," he replied, with a practiced sincerity.

Fran came back to the table with a wooden bowl of pickles, cup of coffee, plate of creamer packages and sugar. "Hi, Doll. You made it. We've been waiting for you." She winked at Mandy.

"Ready to order?"

Jack replied with ease, as if he were talking to a favorite aunt, "Sorry to have kept you waiting, Fran. I'll take a coffee, too. And corned beef on rye, with a cup of matzo ball soup... and Mandy, you wanted the same, or something else?"

"Sure. Yeah, I'll have the same." That eliminated the need to focus on the menu, which was so jumbled and huge and hard to process when she felt so nervous and distracted. A guy who takes charge. How refreshing, she thought. He could plan our vacations, research mortgage rates, decide what color to paint the baby's... STOP. Don't go there, Mandy. You're setting yourself up for disappointment.

"So, I would think you'd meet a bunch of women at your shows," she said coyly.

"I meet a lot of girls at my shows," he replied with a shrug.

Did he mean "Yes, I do meet a lot of women at my shows"? Or did he mean, "I meet a lot of girls" as opposed to *women*?

"And? So?" Mandy was hoping he'd expound on what he'd said, without her having to ask for elaboration.

"So... why am I doing online dating? I've already fucked them all."

SCREECH. CRASH. BANG.

Was he joking? Even if he was, was that an okay thing to say on a first date? Is crassness funny when it's unexpected?

He answered her thoughts with, "Sorry. Not funny. I was... just joking."

PHEW.

He continued: "My therapist says I sabotage things with crude jokes, as a defense mechanism."

Okay, so, nobody's perfect.

"It's one of the reasons things didn't work out with my ex -- well, almost ex -- wife."

Too much. Too much. The corned beef hadn't even come yet.

"Plus, she kept pushing for the house with the picket fence and kids and all."

Mandy didn't know what to say. How to fix this. Get him off this line of conversation. At least for now.

"Oh, gawd," she finally let out. "And you probably want to just enjoy life, play your music... I'm like that with my acting. I mean, we're only mid-thirties, right? 40's the new 30, as they say. Heh heh."

"Totally." Did she catch a sparkle in his eye?

Just then Fran returned with cups of soup, a lone matzo ball filling each one like a whale in a bathtub. Mandy hated matzo ball soup.

"Sorry, Kids. Bad news. No more corned beef today. Second choice?"

"Shoot. I don't know. What do you want, Mandy?"

Mandy didn't know, either. "I'm... not sure."

Fran walked away and returned with two gigantic, overpopulated menus.

"Well, take your time. We ain't going nowhere. We're open 24 hours."

INVISIBLE

Doby was tired of chores.

Seemed like everyone else got to do what they wanted to do. Father worked. Mother played Mahjong with her lady friends. Doby watched from the screened in porch as big sister Phoebe played with a group of girls. He couldn't hear their words. Only that they were punctuated with spurts of laughter. Jack, the terrier-mix mutt, sat in a spot of sun with his eyes closed. Even Jack got to do what he wanted to do.

Doby was sick and tired of doing chores. Or rather, Doby was sick. Being sick made him tired. And doing the things he was told he had to do to stay alive felt like a chore. When he told Mother or Father how he felt, they said "Life has rules. Every person, place or thing – we all have to follow rules. You're not the only one." But to Doby, it seemed like the rules were uneven.

There were two rules he hated most. Rule #1 - Don't go out in the sun. Rule #2 – Don't get overheated. Today was a hot day. He wished it were grey.

Mother tried. Earlier in the day she said, "honey, if you want I can skip Mahjong? Stay home with you and play Parcheesi? Maybe Monopoly?"

Doby did not want to be pitied. Doby wanted to play with someone other than Mother for a change. Phoebe never offered to stay inside. She knew better – as if hanging around him too much might cause her to catch it and be trapped inside forever. Phoebe was the complete opposite of Doby. Hours in the sun had turned her skin golden brown. Her blond hair had streaks of golden highlights that radiated in the sun. She painted her fingers and toes bright colors to match her clothes.

Doby was pale. His hair was ashen colored and dingy from lack of fresh air. Sometimes he lay on the floor with Jack, the tip of his foot in the sun.

Phoebe purposefully played in the farthest corner of the yard. This was the conclusion Doby came to today. She could have brought the girls over to this side. Closer to the porch or even inside the porch. Instead, she chose to be far away. Doby squinted his eyes hard and sent her an unspoken message. I'm coming for you.

Doby noticed that just on the other side of the gaggle of girls was a patch of shade from the neighbor's garage. I need to get there, he thought. He ripped a sheet of paper out of his pastel drawing book and started to plan.

He drew DaVinci-like drawings of the position of the sun, and its relationship to the roof of the garage. Where would it be in twenty minutes? An hour? He made a playbook of tactical moves that would get him to the shady oasis in the fewest number of steps, without being harassed by Phoebe or spotted by Old Mrs. Dunphy, who would surely tell Mother.

He made a supply list and retreated into the house to start searching for his "rescue items".

Doby would get there. He couldn't live on the porch forever. Even Mother and Father had to understand that.

He slipped on his protective clothing -- head-to-toe coverage --

and knew instantly he was disobeying Rule #2. He felt exhilarated... and overheated. He grabbed Items #1 and #2 -- an umbrella and a spray bottle, filled with water and ready for action. He opened the third item -- an old white sheet, with Jack's bite marks and other unidentifiable stains. This would be his parachute-canopy-cover-up, with the umbrella as back-up. He slung the binoculars around his neck, focusing them on his sister's friend Jane. She had a pretty smile and freckles and sometimes said "hello" to him when she came in to get a drink of water or use the bathroom.

Doby was ready to make his move. The patch of shade was getting smaller. Time was of the essence. He reviewed his playbook one last time. He took a deep breath and glanced toward the front door, to make sure Mother wasn't about to put a damper on his plans.

With the parachute billowing above him, Doby ran. He ran to Station 1, the garbage bins overflowing with big brown bags. Jack came barking alongside him. This was a triumph to him, as well, it seemed.

Doby set his sights on Station 2, the withered Plum Tree that no longer offered shade. He would have to run around the old picnic bench, or hurdle over it, but he lacked faith in his nimbleness. He went around and made it to the tree, sweat dripping off his brow.

Darn. He forgot the last item on his supply list -- his can of ice-cold pop. An important item. Crucial, even.

He looked at his destination. He looked back at the house. Equal distance to each. If only he weren't so hot. And uncomfortable.

Spray bottle. He had the spray bottle in his knapsack. He pulled it out and doused his face, then opened his mouth and generously sprayed.

Phew. Mission not aborted. Mission continued. One last, long leg and he'd be there: Paradise. Suddenly, Phoebe noticed him and started to run over. She had that smug, self-righteous look she sometimes got. She would not win this one. Doby was not going to surrender. No way. Not now. Not when he was this close.

Doby and Jack started running toward the shady spot with the abandon of a prisoner set free, and a terrier with nothing better to do. He heard Phoebe yelling his name. He heard her making tattletale threats. He even heard Mother's car pulling up in front of the house.

And still he ran. He could not bring himself to stop running. He had broken the rules and would certainly pay the price. But YES, it was worth it.

LONELINESS

(ADAPTED INTO THE PLAY "PUSS IN: BOOTY CALL")

♡

It was just a chicken pot pie. The same she'd eaten every Monday night for as long as she could remember. But something snapped in her tonight. A despondency so deep that every mouthful brought greater and louder wails, until she could hear the neighbor pounding on the kitchen wall between them.

She grabbed her remote and turned up the volume on *The Big Bang Theory*. She looked down at her chipped purple toenail polish and wished she'd remembered to pick up the remover at the Walgreens across the street. It seemed too far away now: going downstairs too big of a venture.

She glanced at Carmine the Cat and picked up her cell phone.

"Come over." She texted. She did not hit "Send". She put the phone down. Carried her plate to the kitchen and banged on the wall, for good measure. She picked up the phone and hit "Send".

She went to her bedroom and slipped off her Innie-Outies, the yoga pants that could, *in theory*, be worn outside, in public. She looked for something that would appear accidentally sexy. She opted for the jeans -- the ones he'd commented on that time at the cafe -- and fought back tears as she put them on. She paired them with a form-fitting Wilco "ringer" T-shirt: a well-known winner with the lads.

She went to the living room and checked her phone. Relief washed over her as she realized he'd returned her text: "I thought you didn't want to do this anymore?" Winky emoji.

"I don't", she texted.

Then -- so he wouldn't get the wrong idea -- she texted back: "But isn't that what makes it so... enticing?" Winky emoji.

She went to the bathroom to fill in the chips on her neglected toenails. As she shut the medicine cabinet, she caught her reflection in the mirror and began, again, to sob. Quietly this time.

Carmine the Cat came in to check on her. He rubbed up against the back of her calves. Funny, she thought, he always seemed to know when she needed comforting. She felt bad locking him in the bathroom. She tidied the house while she waited.

Her text came in a bit past 7, as Scott was sitting down with his laptop to work on his resume. He had started working odd jobs in college and liked the freelance lifestyle. And the perks!

"Come over" is all the text had said. He hadn't wanted to seem too eager in his response. She was at least ten years older than he was, and a good twenty over his other girlfriends.

Girlfriend? Did he just label her girlfriend? He laughed to himself. Definitely not girlfriend. Employer? Friend with Benefits? He wondered if he should bring something with him? Stop at the Corner Stop for a bottle of wine? He typed in "Wine?" and then deleted it. He typed "On my way" before deleting that too.

Honestly, the way the last visit went he didn't think he'd see her again. He did like her. Even though she was overly emotional. She could be funny too. But when she got angry, he could see why she still lived alone. Dressed in his new imitation army jacket and Diesel jeans, he hopped on the subway to make his way to her place uptown. He hadn't shaved.

Less than one hour after sending the text, the downstairs doorbell rang and she buzzed him in. It was a quick walk up, unless you got caught in a conversation with Mrs. Huber, the building manager, on the 3rd floor landing.

Carmine the Cat crouched low with his nose up against the bathroom door. He was god-damn tired of her shenanigans. Really. He was on his last life with it.

She opened the front door and exuberantly greeted her visitor Scott. Carmine waited to hear Scott's response back but it was low and muffled.

They walked into the living room and sat close together on the couch. She laughed. It sounded fake. And flirtatious.

How much more can a cat give, Carmine wondered? He strode across the chenille bath mat and pulled out a few tufts of cotton for good measure. It felt good - but the feeling passed. He hopped onto the toilet seat and jumped up to the sink. He knocked over the toothbrush holder and pushed the soap dish into the trash can. A sense of accomplishment overtook him.

Feeling tired, he pulled her terry cloth bathrobe onto the floor and fell asleep. In dreams, theirs was a perfect relationship. Spooning together on the couch. Licking the pot pie bowl. Running from room to room, chasing spirits.

When he woke up it was still dark outside and the apartment was quiet. When will she release me? He thought about throwing himself against the door. Too much effort. He slid his paws underneath for good measure.

Finally she came to get him. Picked him up and held him close. She started to cry. He didn't care. They were alone together again. He burrowed into her neck. Purred.

In the kitchen, she poured cereal into a ceramic bowl and filled it with milk. He sat on the tabletop, swinging his tail, waiting for his turn.

BLUE

I decided we were making a ritual. Sara and Julie looked at each other and rolled their eyes. Then without saying anything, they both turned and started walking away down Greene Street. I stood there stunned and surprised. I watched them walk past the Robinson's house and then Mrs. Kelsey's place.

"Guys! Guys, answer me!"

By the time I realized they were actually not going to stop, they were half a block away. Almost to the point where Sara would turn right to go to her house and Julie would go left. I shouted three simple life changing words, panting, half out of breath running up behind them.

"I'll... Do... Anything!"

They both stopped short and turned.

"I'll do it then," said Sara matter of fact.

"Me too", Julie said. Smiling.

Then we group hugged, reunited from our short estrangement. That night, as I lay in bed with my windows wide open, warm air circulating from the fan overhead, I remember feeling exhilarated. And scared.

The next morning at breakfast, mother asked me what my plans were for the day.

"Um. Gonna hang out with the girls."

"Going?"

"What?'

"The word is going? There is no such word as 'gonna'."

"Right. I'm GOING to."

"Sara and Julie?"

"Yep."

"Whatcha girls doing?"

"Riding our bikes over to the beach for a bit. Then maybe baking cookies at Jules."

At this point I would normally have pointed out that there is no such word as 'whatcha', but I don't. Not because I'm a good, respectful daughter who listens to her mother. But because I did not want to draw unnecessary attention to myself. Not that morning. And I most certainly didn't want to get stuck at home so mother could make a point by having me spend the day helping her with chores.

I smiled. Mother seemed happy with my response and sent me off with well wishes for the day. I grabbed my beach bag, my purple Schwinn bike with the pink tassels on the handlebars and a crumpled up $5 bill from the pile of loose money on the dining room table.

I rode fast down the sidewalk to Sara's house. Then the two of us rode down the alley to pick up Jules. We were all so excited we could barely speak. The azaleas were in bloom and the sun was already high and hot in the day.

At this point, you are probably thinking that we are on a perilous path requiring course correction. Let me assure you that our plan was what most would consider childhood foolishness back in the seventies. And perfectly normal for kids to do today 40 years later. But being good girls, who up until that point had never done anything without prior parental approval, it felt like we were on the precipice of living life out of bounds.

We rode and rode with childhood immunity to the muggy heat of the day. Our sense of purpose and courage building with each block behind us. Beyond the neighborhood cul de sacs and winding streets without sidewalks. Past the golf course framed on both sides by tall forest. The local TV station and it's lettered white van parked out front waiting to be dispatched to cover anything that might happen. Into downtown and the brick storefronts. The hardware store, Elliot's drug store and the Christian Science Reading Room.

We stopped at the river. We had run out of road. Far enough though from home. We set ourselves up on a flowered twin sheet Jules brought in her backpack. She had taken it off her bed that morning. It would end up dirty with grass stains that wouldn't wash out. She had also brought a hand mirror, a hairbrush, and a pair of small nail scissors. The kind you trim loose threads with. I brought the $5 so we could stop for ice cream on the way back to celebrate our day. I took it out and laid it on the sheet alongside the other offerings.

"TA DA!" said Sara. She takes a bottle of fingernail polish out of her front pocket. Dragon red. She places it in the center of the sheet.

"Who's first?" Jules asked.

"I'll go first." I said this in an attempt to redeem myself from the day before. Last one in, first one out so to speak.

"Fine by me" said Sara.

"You do the nails. I'll do the hair." Said Jules.

And the first transformation began. Sara painted my fingernails and toes one by one, as if creating an American masterpiece.

"Let's all do bangs and bobs" said Jules.

"Let's!" I agreed. Nervously. Being the first one and all.

"Absolutely!" Sara said enthusiastically.

Fifteen minutes later, I had changed from my simple seven-year old self to glamour and sophistication. Sure there were spots where I had more red nail polish on my skin than my nails. And my bangs were not exactly straight – but neither were the two sides of my hair. But I definitely felt older. The three of us put our heads close together and looked into our reflection in the hand held mirror and agreed. Job well done.

"Who's next?" I asked.

"I'll go next", said Jules. "Unless you want to Sara?"

"I don't mind. I can go last. Let me do hair this time though."

We all got up and switched places. As if our places on the sheet somehow designated our specific role in the ritual.

I started painting Jules' nails. Halfway thru the first hand, we heard it.

"Was that lightning?" asked Sara.

"I hope not," said Jules.

BOOM. Thunder. Followed by more lightning.

"It's okay, let's keep going" I said. I started to work on finger number four. Sara snipped a three-inch piece off the back of Jules' hair.

BOOM, CLAP, BOOM, CLAP. Suddenly the sky opened up. Rain started pouring down.

We grabbed everything and crammed it into Jules' backpack. I was the first one on my bike and started riding towards home. Sara and Julie followed closely behind. The farther we rode, the harder it rained. None of us stopped to say goodbye. Each one of us veering off for cover as we got closer to our homes.

By the time I got home and dumped my bike by the back door, I was soaked and had all but forgotten about my new hairstyle and racy adult-looking fingernails. I stood dripping water on the kitchen floor.

"My gosh. What happened to you?" Mary, our maid, stood in

the kitchen with her cutting board full of chopped vegetables and a crock pot waiting to be filled.

"Rain." I said.

"That's obvious. I'm talking about your hair. Your lovely hair. And what happened to your nails? Your Mama's going to kill you."

"Oh. Yeah. Well."

"Looks like you've been rummaging around in a dead possum's belly and now you've got blood stains all over your hands. I hope you didn't pay anyone to do that."

"I didn't." Mary's response was a different take on how Sara, Jules and I had viewed things not more than a half hour ago.

"Well, now in all seriousness. What happened?"

"I had a makeover."

"I'd say you did."

I wondered at what point she'd come over and wrap me in a towel and tell me not to worry and let me make you a cup of warm tea to dry your bones?

"Who else had this makeover?"

"Sara. And Jules. Only it started raining so they couldn't get theirs finished."

"Praise god were they lucky." She said.

"Well, you better go upstairs and dry yourself off. I can try to clean up your hands before your Mother gets home. I'm not sure there is anything we can do about that hair though. You better hope she's in a good mood when she gets here."

I did get in trouble, but it wasn't as bad as it should have been. By the time Mary and Mother were finished laughing about it downstairs, my reveal packed a lot less punch. And the hair eventually came back as hair does.

It's June 5th and I'm standing in the reception area of Country Villa West. It's funny how we all ended up in different places. Physically, geographically, spiritually. I haven't seen Sara in about twenty years. She lives in Florida with three kids. We mostly stayed in touch through letters here and there, which then gave way to Facebook posts. I am nervous and excited to see her. I wonder how much she's changed and what she will think of my transformation into an adult. I live in New York, having moved there for an entry level job that turned into a career. I always seem to be in and out of relationships. Two years seems to be my max.

Jules got married and moved to L.A. The marriage lasted five years. She had always been the one growing up who wanted kids, but she never had any. For a while I heard she was having an affair with a married man. If we had been in touch during that time, I can assure you I would not have approved. But I probably wouldn't have said anything. I recognize Sara the moment she walks through the automatic double glass doors.

"HELL-O" she says, walking past the seating area with a painting of mallards flying over a marsh.

"Hi there! How was your flight?"

"Fine. Fine. Yours?"

"Uneventful. Good."

"I'm glad."

"Have you seen Jules yet?"

"No, I was waiting for you."

"I love it. A reuniting of the threesome. Did you stop and pick up the list?"

"I did."

We ask the woman behind the desk to direct us to 201B. She points us down the hall, past the solarium to the west wing of the building. We set off, walking what seems to be endless hallways.

We knock on the door and Jules' voice hollers back "Come on in!".

Jules is sitting up in bed. By the window is a brown leather chair. The sun is coming through the window. Beyond the window, a parking lot. Empty and chained off. Weeds and wildflowers poking thru the cement when they get a chance.

"Well hello there, ladies!"

"Hello to you." Both Sara and I say back.

"You know you didn't have to come. But I love that you did."

"We've brought accoutrements." I say.

"And snacks", says Sara.

The hospice nurse knocks on the door and peaks in.

"I wanted to see if you needed anything before I go on break."

"No, I'm good thank you" Jules says. These are my friends from... well, from different parts now but we all grew up together."

"How wonderful. Enjoy!" The hospice nurse leaves for break. Grabs her paperback book, Snickers from the vending machine, and sits on the ground in the shaded corner of the abandoned parking lot.

"First things first", I say.

Out of my tote bag I pull a hairbrush, blow dryer and a pair of real hair cutting scissors. Sara takes a small paper bag out of her purse. We line everything up on top of the sheet at the end of Jules' bed.

"Really you guys." Jules says.

"No, really." Says Sara.

Sara and I take turns cutting, styling and blow-drying Jules' hair. In less than 10 minutes, it actually looks really good.

"Who would have thought?" says Jules.

Sara and I look at each other and start laughing.

"At least it's not crooked" I say.

"Next!" Sara opens the brown paper bag and pulls out nail polish remover, cuticle nippers, emery board and file. Then the nail polish.

"It's Blue!" shouts Jules. "What happened to fire breathing dragon red?"

"Red's for old people" says Sara. "All the young kids now are wearing blue."

"I sometimes wear blue," I say.

"Who's first?" asks Sara.

"Not me. I went first last time, remember?"

"I should go first." Says Jules. "I never know how much time I have these days."

I say, "Or when the sky's going to open up and just downright pour."

Sara and I stay in L.A. a little less than a week. Each day we see Jules and reminisce about all of the things we had done together. We leave with a renewed urgency to see each other, so Sara comes up to New York the next month for a visit. We mostly talk about Jules. Had she changed, had she done all of the things she wanted to do, had we?

We both agree that we were glad we had taken the time to see her. Or see her off, as it would be. By the end of that summer Jules is gone, and things in my life go back to normal, or as normal as life can be.

SUMMER SESSIONS

♡

I decided we were making a ritual. It just felt like it. Like something we'd be doing over and over. Again and again. Something that would mark the beginning of summer. The beginning of a temporary and fleeting freedom. The beginning of an exciting future yet to behold... until school started, at least. What I didn't realize was how meaningful it would be. And how, in the end, it really had little to do with the future at all.

Ginger, Jane and I had brought our sleeping bags into the back yard, along with Mom's upholstered green rocking chairs and wobbly ring-stained coffee table, and thereupon we created an outdoor utopia: a space where bedtime could be put off until further notice and eight-year-olds could sip hot cocoa under the stars.

The sun had just set, and it was still warm enough for short sleeves. It felt like 5:00 but was closer to 8:30. Mom had lost track of time, so we were in the clear. She was on a long-distance call to Frankie, and we knew she wouldn't be bugging us for at least a couple more hours.

The first night, we pulled out our portable plastic record player. The one we'd gotten two Christmases ago, when all our friends had gotten real stereos with cassette players and detached speakers. We listened to Dad's old albums: Best of Bread and Rumors and Jim Croce. Someone --- Ginger? -- named it The Summer Sessions, and we laughed and laughed. We snuck See's suckers from Mom's special stash on top of the fridge... and when we finished them, the sticks became cigarettes, though the soggy paper started to come apart on our tongues.

It wasn't until way past eleven that Mom came out, with that feigned look of disapproval that we knew was disguised pride at how clever her girls were. We knew, too, that she would have preferred to join us right there on her favorite thrift store quilt, rather than having to force us to brush teeth and "Go straight to bed!"

A couple of nights later, we did it again. This time, it evolved into a kind of crafting party. We still had the tunes, and the warm drinks, but we also made God's Eyes... and played Cat's Cradle with the leftover yarn. We made cardboard telescopes out of paper towel rolls and looked for constellations, and when we found them, we sang them songs. "Ol' Orion, I am cryin' over you-ou-ou..."

And we did it the next night. And the night after that. And the next.

These Summer Sessions had become something we'd plan our days around, thinking up new ideas to make them better, going through the motions of day camp but dreaming of dusk. We didn't tell anyone outside the family about it. It was our special thing. We ended up foregoing friends' sleepover parties, special roller rink events in town... hell, we even skipped out on Battle of the Network Stars to be outside under the real stars.

Then, one night, Mom did join us. We had pulled out the Super 8 projector -- with a very long extension cord -- and were watching old home movies on the side of Crazy Bill's garage that abutted our yard. She was carrying a plate of buttery cinnamon toast, and her eyes were riveted on the projection. We pounced on that plate and pretended not to notice the tears running down her face. We teased

Jane for never wearing a shirt in those movies, called her Naked Nudie, and made bets about how many items of clothing she'd have on in the next reel. One reel was labeled "Zoo" but actually ended up mostly being Dad chasing us kids around this very backyard with a hose, our silent squeals easily imaginable, despite the clicking of the film through the projector. Man, this was the pinnacle, for sure!

By the end of that summer, we must have listened to those records and watched those movies fifty times. Yet we knew there'd be more times, because we knew we needed them. We had, indeed, created a ritual out there, in our forsaken, overgrown backyard. And this ritual was a way for us to remember happier times, to finally grieve together, and to pick up some of the pieces, even. Though we never did make any mention of that one 4th of July party, or its last empty can of beer, or that busted-up VW bug that busted up our family.

COOKIES & DREAMS

♡♡

The first batch of cookies. That's how the fight started. Weasel put them in the trash. I took them out, wrapped them in cellophane and left. It was still dark out when I pulled away from the curb to drive across town. I could hear Weasel yelling from the front porch.

I drove half a mile. Turned on the radio. Phoebe Snow was singing, killing me softly with his song. "I heard he sang a good song, I heard he had a style..." I sang along, then felt sad. I turned the dial looking for a happier song but it was too early. On the news station they were talking about weather. "Expect tornadoes throughout the valley".

"My life is a tornado," I said back. It's silly, cause now I'm talking out loud to nobody at all. I wonder if that's how grandma ended up on Prozac living in a halfway house outside of town. After her scrambled eggs breakdown. Grandpa got his head split open with a metal spatula. I'm headed to see him now.

Sixth street was completely dark except for the all-night tattoo parlor. I felt the urge to stop. It's not hard to imagine. Me with a tattoo. Weasel brought me in the last time. And I put his name on my shoulder. Even though my long hair mostly covers it. "Now you can't be buried in the Jewish cemetery. Better not tell Grandma."

Grandpa said. It's funny because he doesn't even blame her for the attack. He calls it an accident. But the authorities won't let Grandma come home.

"What do you want?" The tattoo guy was young enough to be my son.

This question has come up before. Last time I hesitated, and Weasel yelled out "Weasel!". I'm doing whatever I want from now on. I got a little hummingbird on my ankle. We took a shot of brandy together to dull the pain.

It's still too early to be at Grandpa's house. All the lights are off, except for I can see through the crack in the curtains the glow of the TV in the living room. And Grandpa asleep, half sitting up on the couch. I leave the cookies on the porch. Use my lipstick to make a heart and write my name on a piece of paper towel. Then I worry that someone might come by and swipe them. Or a critter might eat them. So I pick them back up again.

I start the car. A tornado has touched down by Emmet's Field. The sun is rising. I decide to head home while it's still safe. Weasel's waiting with a fresh batch of cookies for breakfast when I arrive.

COOKIEGATE

♡

Inspired by true events on The Great British Bake Off

INTERVIEWER: The first batch of cookies came out perfectly.

ME: Yes. The first batch of cookies came out perfectly. I think I could have won the whole thing with those.

INTERVIEWER: Then what happened? Walk us through it.

ME: Well, so, the cookies – technically, they were rugelach... rugelach... raspberry/walnut rugelach. Anyway, as you saw on the show, they needed to chill for AT LEAST thirty minutes. At least. In this competition, you have to make adjustments, so you can't really let something chill or proof for the optimum amount of time. So, I put the second batch in the fridge immediately, thinking my timing would work well.

INTERVIEWER: And what happened?

ME: Well, you saw. They were taken out. They sat out on the counter, in 100 degree weather, instead.

INTERVIEWER: And – not naming names, but one of the other contestants took them out?

ME: Yeah. To make room for hers. Apparently. She forgot that she took mine out, meant to put them back in front, and didn't.

INTERVIEWER: It's not hard to imagine the anger you must have felt when you realized what was going on.

ME: Well, yeah. You could see it on my face in the tape. But, I was really more in a state of shock. And it was so hot. And you're so stressed, and everything is so surreal during the weeks of competing. One round after the other. Little sleep. Adrenaline and personality clashing.

INTERVIEWER: So... you threw them away?

ME: I threw them away. I just took the whole tray and dumped it... And walked off set.

INTERVIEWER: And forfeited.

ME: I didn't have time to make another batch, and you can't win without the exact amount, all uniform and perfect. I knew I'd lost.

INTERVIEWER: And what about – well, everybody has seen the show already. What about Tina? Did she feel bad? Did she apologize?

ME I don't blame her. It was an honest mistake. But the internet sure blamed her. The blogosphere went wild. Made death threats. There was speculation that she knew all along what she was doing.

INTERVIEWER: And many out there – even the judges – are saying you still could have won, had you not done that. Had you just made the second batch as they were. Or gave them the first batch only to judge. What about that? Do you wish you could take back what you did? That split-second decision?

ME: This question has come up before. Obviously. I've replayed that moment in my mind over and over. Regret is an evil monster. It's a lot easier to just move on. I wish it had never happened. But, it did. And I did what I did. And that's just... that's just how the cook -- well, that's just how it goes.

THE WONDER OF IT ALL

♡♡

PERSON: John, late 30's, father-to-be. Hasn't told anyone yet

PLACE: Las Vegas, bachelor party weekend

THING: A baseball bat

♡

John was in serious trouble. Patron-Silver-induced trouble. The random business card, raging headache and mangled baseball bat at his feet weren't the half of it. It was the fresh tattoo "Wanda" across his chest that really worried him.

They had all joked about the expectations for that weekend. Truth is, their pal Felix liked to gamble. That was it. He had absolutely no intention of having the stereotypical debaucherous Las Vegas Bachelor Party when he suggested it to them all.

They were still planning to saturate his liver with booze, and in turn, lure him to at least one strip club. Especially John. He was always the ringleader. And this time, the stakes were even higher for John, since both his thirties and his freedom were drifting away from him.

He hadn't yet mentioned his impending fatherhood: the Tat Pack already teased him for being "whupped". Maybe now that Felix was getting married, too, they'd let up a bit on that. Damn, had that irritated him. They'd always considered John to be the Wild One, the daredevil. He never minded it and even wanted to maintain that reputation.

So, hours into the casino stint, when Felix was in the hole by almost a grand, John knew it was time to move in. He gathered the other guys -- Jason, Leo, Dave -- and whisked the groom-to-be out of the hotel and into the night.

Already three sheets to the wind, they headed straight for the Alibi to see some flesh. The liquor seemed to materialize in their hands the minute they entered, and de-materialize almost as quickly. Leo -- Mister Moneybags -- was the one who moved them onto the Patron, ordering two bottles without consultation. John didn't complain. No one did.

Felix sat uncomfortably in front of a half-clad blonde woman, who had heard he was the bachelor of honor. Leo and Dave disappeared for a time, Jason found a female "friend", and John kept knocking back the drinks, watching the ladies and thinking about his future daughter. *What if she ended up in a joint like this?*, he thought. *Would she be empowered, an independent woman in charge of her own body? Would she feel threatened? Would she feel vulnerable, frustrated? Damn, this parenthood thing is a buzzkill.*

The thoughts were too much. He suddenly felt ill and ran to the men's room, barely making it to the toilet bowl.

When he returned, Felix was on his feet, chomping at the bit.

"Can we go now? I'm over this. I'm amped. Let's go do SOMETHING."

"This is something, Feel-Feel. Relax. Go with it."

"Hey. This is my weekend. I wanna get out of here. Go find the guys. Meet me outside."

John found Leo and Dave emerging from a back room. He didn't ask questions. He dragged Jason away from the dark corner, where he seemed to be snuggling with his new friend, and they all joined Felix on the sidewalk in front of the club.

"I want to play some ball," said Felix.

The guys chuckled. A little too hard. But they were down, especially since John was already leading the way and bringing up his Uber app as he sang "Take Me Out to the Ballgame."

When the driver arrived -- a fortysomething Persian man in a spotless Highlander -- John slurred an explanation of the circumstances and requested any leads on a midnight baseball game. Ahmad had none.

Miraculously enough, he did have a lead on an extra baseball bat -- in his trunk -- that he offered to let them borrow, provided they found a way to get it back to him the next morning. At first, they were all floored by this. But things usually worked out serendipitously for John, so he didn't really question it. Leo suggested that most Uber drivers probably carried some sort of weapon for security's sake.

Ahmad gave them a business card, and they made arrangements to email him with a meeting-up place for the bat return. He dropped them off in an empty field, a sort of lot, overgrown with weeds.

"This is PERFECT", said Felix.

"WONDROUS", agreed John.

"If you build it, they will come," said Jason, to a pummeling from the rest of the guys.

They had the field. Now, they needed bases. Leo created first base, with his grey hoodie. An old tire became second. An empty propane tank served as a marker for third. And home was where

Dave sat, almost catatonic with fatigue and the beginnings of a drug comedown.

They broke into teams and set up to start the game. This was what Felix wanted all along. Some gambling, some sports, some guy time.

"I'll pitch," John said. Then, he remarked, synapses catching up, "We have no fucking ball."

Under other circumstances, the Tat Pack would have been irritated by this revelation, angry even. This time, though, they all laughed as if it were the funniest damned thing ever. Ha! No ball! They had a Wonder Bat, a perfect playing field, makeshift bases, and NO BALL.

"No ball -- just like you, Jason!" Leo burst out, and they all fell to the ground with the hilariousness of it all.

Jason, though laughing, feigned rage and started batting at the propane tank, which managed to dent Ahmad's bat.

"Fuuuuck," lamented John. "Ahmad's bat, Dude!"

"Bring it", said Felix. "Let's bounce."

"Bounce! Ha ha! Let's see this propane tank bounce!"

With Jason's proclamation came more denting of the bat, and John started worrying about broken Uber promises.

"Knock it off, J." Then, to get him to do so, he said the only thing he knew could derail him: "Dudes. Let's go get tattoos!"

They decided NOT to contact Ahmad at this time. Ordering another Uber, they discussed the idea of getting matching bachelor party tattoos, something to commemorate the occasion. Someone suggested "Felix '17" to a round of naes. Someone else came up with "No Ball" to an obvious round of groans and naes (the loudest among them, Jason.)

Then, John became sentimental... it often happened when he drank. But at this juncture in his life, when he had this impending baby and parenthood and enormous life change happening, it washed over him like no other tequila mawkishness. He shouted out "Wonder! Let's write 'wonder'!"

Now, the morning after, in his overly-air-conditioned hotel room, he suddenly remembered all this. And in the hungover light of day, he realized "wonder" would have been bad enough, but "Wanda" was a damn near threat to his marriage, an undeserved one at that.

He went to the bathroom sink, splashed cold water on his face, then sat back down on the floor, his aching back up against the bed.

What to do? What to do?

His cell phone was ringing, but he couldn't bring himself to answer it. Too tired and deflated to do anything else, he picked up Ahmad's destroyed bat and cradled it in his arms.

THE FIDGET SPINSTER

PERSON: Miss Marjorie Withers - former prima ballerina, in her 70s, a bit of a Miss Havisham feel to her

PLACE: On a group safari in Africa, with a bunch of other English and American tourists

THING: A fidget spinner which she received from her great-nephew as a parting gift

"Trip of a Lifetime" it read, and Miss Marjorie Withers already felt like this trip was going to deliver. Cece, her dear friend since they'd met decades ago as dancers in The London Ballet company, had sent her the brochure.

Cece was a Yankee through and through. She never found occasion to dress appropriately in a skirt or dress. Not even for church! "Always dress like it's the best day of your life", Miss Marjorie frequently told herself. Oh well, to each her own. Usually it took Miss Marjorie long stretches of time to make decisions involving finances, but this time she didn't think twice about spending the money and jumped at the chance to travel with her dear friend.

The brochure continued "No trip to South America would be complete with the opportunity to learn more about the local tribes and wildlife! Travel to Dumazulu Village and learn about daily life for the Zulu tribe, renowned for its warrior culture. You'll witness traditional tribal dancing and ceremonial beer drinking. In Swaziland, you can search colorful markets and see the basket weavers. Then you will continue on to Kruger National Park, South Africa's premier game sanctuary where surely you will spot the "Big Five" – lions, elephants, buffalo, rhino and the more elusive leopards".

Cece had fallen asleep with her head resting on the bus window. The bus was evenly split - half Brits, half Americans. Everyone segregated into couples and foursomes. Cece and me were the only mixed pair. How strange we must seem, indeed. Hee hee. She chuckled just loud enough that the woman across the aisle glanced her way and smiled.

She herself, Miss Marjorie, was tall and thin. Well put together, nicely dressed for a woman her age. Hair pulled back in a simple bun. Special wardrobe expressly purchased for the safari. She had followed the recommended packing instructions to a tee - sunscreen, tissue packs, mosquito repellant with DEET, umbrella. She had packed a notebook for starting her memoir, a pocket Bible, pencil and pencil sharpener, plus a turbo glow fidget spinner her great nephew Simon gave her as a parting gift.

Cece, on the other hand, had not prepared herself at all it seemed. In fact, she rather looked quite the same as she always did. Wild frizzy gray hair. Worn blue jeans meant for day laborers not aging ballerinas on safari. Sandals. Obviously she had not heeded the warnings about wild animals and exposed toes. She had packed dangling earrings and lip gloss. Miss Marjorie shook her head and reached down unconsciously to tie her sneakers.

The bus lurched first to the left and then back to the right throwing everyone to and fro. Mason, the fourth year college student from Boston, ended up in Marjorie's lap for half a second before he was sent sailing back to his original spot. Everyone hollered more from the surprise of it than anything else. Then came a loud shishing or shooshing sound before the bus came to a complete stop.

"I dreamt that a handsome suitor grazed my cheek" Cece said.

"You hitchhiked a ride on my daydream" Miss Marjorie retorted. Causing them both to burst out laughing.

"British laughter... the best medicine" chimed in Sam, the middle-aged beekeeper from Vermont. He took a swig from his flask. The women traded glances. He had tried to strike up a conversation earlier with Cece about the perils of his job. She had not been interested.

"Ladies and gentlemen, we are going to have to clear the bus I'm afraid. Flat tire." The driver hollered out over the shishing sound.

The bus didn't have a spare tire, so they all sat around atop their luggage waiting for the replacement bus. Miss Marjorie took out her binoculars to look for wildlife. Sam tried once again to strike up a conversation with Cece. He must think she's a country bumpkin, thought Marjorie. After an hour or so, one of their fellow tourists began rummaging through their bags for water and something to eat which caused everyone else to start scurrying about. Marjorie and Cece looked over the horizon nibbling nuts and seeds.

As the next town was many hours away, the travelers waited for quite some time.

"Should only be a few more hours. Thank you for your patience". The driver himself had quite a spread of savory snacks.

"No doubt this is not the first time this has happened." Miss Marjorie commented.

"Indeed" Cece concurred.

Finally, a bus emerged from the dust. Everyone stood and waived.

The Americans jumped up and down cheering. The Brits happily nodded patting each other on the back. The bus came to a halt directly behind their bus. However within moments it became clear the bus was not intended for them as it already had a full passenger load. But the Americans were causing such a commotion the wrong bus thought it should stop.

The side of the bus read "Zimbabwe National Baseball." On the bus sat the entire Zimbabwe National Baseball team plus their manager. They watched as the tourists switched from jubilation to total let down. The team was on their way home from a winning game and didn't want to be the cause of these strangers' sadness. Taking a team vote, they decided to exit the bus and greet the visitors.

Not being a sports person, although one had to be the ultimate athlete to dance, Miss Marjorie did not notice who struck up the impromptu baseball game until the first ball was hit and Beekeeper Sam started running past the makeshift ice chest bases. It was starting to get late in the day. Nobody except Cece and she seemed to mind the further delay.

"Do you think we will wind up sleeping on the bus?" Cece asked.

"That would not be the type of adventure I had hoped for" Marjorie quipped back.

Her patience wearing thin Miss Marjorie reached down into her bag for a lozenge and instead found Simon's fidget spinner. This thing, she thought. Simon thought it a humorous gift after all of her nagging every time he saw her to "stop that incessant spinning". Well, I have good hand-eye coordination, she thought. So she started spinning. Spinning, spinning, spinning... spinning, spinning, spinning. Before she knew it, she had a good rhythm going and she discovered she could spin her fidget spinner and spin her body at the same time. She started dancing about which of course made Cece dance about too.

The Zimbabwe baseball players, distracted by the flurry of movement coming from the two old performers, dropped their gloves and moved towards the activity. Team tourist had no choice but to follow their lead over to where Cece and Miss Marjorie spun. Soon everyone started clapping out the rhythm and several of the players started dancing.

"What is that?" Zimbabwe's pitcher Takunda shouted over the din of clapping and dancing. He pointed at Miss Marjorie's hand.

"This is my fidget spinner!"

"Fidget...."

"SPINNER!!!"

"It is amazing!" Takunda said. "I must have one!"

Miss Marjorie stopped spinning. Cece nearly tumbled into her.

"I must... have a BUS!" Marjorie exclaimed. She gave Takunda a sly look.

"Here. You can take mine." He made a sweeping motion towards their bus.

Miss Marjorie made the trade and the tourists boarded the Zimbabwe National Baseball team bus finally headed to their destination.

As they pulled away, Marjorie watched out the back window as Takunda and the rest of the team took turns with the fidget spinner. On the bus, the Americans AND Brits cheered Marjorie for ostensibly saving the day. Everyone sat intermingled. Cece decided to sit next to Sam.

The Zimbabweans watched the sunset, enjoyed a few Aero bars and Walkers Crisps, then boarded a replacement bus less than an hour later.

LATCHKEY TRAVELER

♡

PERSON: Pamm, 14-year-old girl, into stuff no parent would want to know about

PLACE: San Fernando Valley, CA

THING: A heart-shaped locket

♡♡

"Pammela. Why are you late again for dinner? I am speaking to you." She's already got food on the table and is sitting there with my little sister Sam. Both watching me. Waiting.

Mom calls me Pammela instead of Pamm when she has something important, or heartwarming, to say. Otherwise it's plain Pamm and yes, I spell my name P-A-M-M. I'm always spelling it for people. When people ask me what the second M stands for, I usually say Millions. Or Millennium. But the truth is I just made it up to be different.

"Why are you late?"

"I missed my train."

"Where were you?"

"With friends."

"What's that around your neck?"

A heart-shaped locket "I found". Half truth. Fingers crossed. Little white lie. I got it at a weird second hand clothing store on Sherman Way in Reseda for less than $10. I liked that it was old looking. Tarnished, with an inscription around the edges "Faith is daring the soul to go beyond what the eyes can see". I also like that it has a P on the back.

I'm late because I ran into problems getting back. But I can't tell Mom that. Everything I am going to tell you started with the locket.

"Pamm, put your device away at the table."

"Pamm, don't slam the door."

"Pamm, help your sister get ready for school."

I don't want you to get the wrong idea. I'm a good kid. I get straight A's. I volunteer and play music. I pretty much do what I'm told. But I'm not what you'd call conventional. I have my own style. It's sort of Ska-inspired – cropped plaid pants, white shirts, black ankle boots or sneakers – that sort of thing. I'm kind of lanky and Mom says I'm a "late bloomer" which is a nice way of saying I don't have boobs yet.

Today is Tuesday the 12th of October, 2042.

Mom is the only person I know who still keeps paper calendars. Today's Dad's 40th birthday. She's got it marked on every calendar in the house. It's been five years since he died. I was nine. Not long after, Mom got a hologram made so she could keep him around all the time. Most days, it still sort of feels like he's here. Hanging around the house. But on his birthday, or on days like their anniversary or around the holidays, it makes Mom sad.

Before we got Dad, I used to think home holograms were creepy. Now they seem more normal. We got Patches the year before Dad died. She's second generation A.I. from Canine Robotics. We all got to pick her (she's medium size with white scruffy hair) but I got to name her. That first year, Dad probably had the most interaction with her of any of us, which is why she really reminds me of him sometimes. Way more than the hologram.

It worries Mom that I don't have a lot of friends. I really don't have any. Not because I don't want them, but because all the kids have been paired up or in groups since 1st grade. Or they're Double V– Virtually Vacant. I didn't make up that term. I read it online. It means 100% digital. So they're either not available in the practical world or not the least bit interested in making a new friend. That's okay. Sometimes I feel very solitary but then I have Patches and we find plenty to do together.

"PAMM..."

"I know!"

"Please. Be on time..."

"I will. Promise! Back for Dad's dinner at 6." And out the door I ran.

On the Level 3 platform, I wait for the E train. It travels east/west across the San Fernando Valley. Express without any stops – in 3.74 seconds flat. You used to have to take the regular train (35 minutes) or drive (47 minutes). Then one day, there were so many cars, traffic stood still for 12 hours. The morning after, the city council agreed to pay for the E train. People left their cars for good, right there in the middle of the road where the traffic had stopped. Then the homeless people moved into the abandoned cars and now they aren't homeless anymore.

I set the alarm on my wristband so I won't be late.

The commuters are already at work, so the train isn't very crowded. The train doesn't have stationary seats. That's how they keep them clean and keep the hobos from sleeping on them. When you stand in front of them with the APP open, the seats materialize. The APP is also good for mapping hobo enclaves and has alerts and notifications when convicted felons or random people you have chosen to "block" are approaching.

Patches and I board the last car. We're the only ones in this section so it's super peaceful and a little eerie. The Promenade Mall/Topanga Canyon/Malibu stop is at the end of the tracks. Then the train heads back the way it came. I switch on the Lorde 30 Years of Greatest Hits playlist and take out my Swiss Army Knife. I've been trying to pry this locket open for two days. It's rusted closed. No matter what I try, it won't budge.

"Next stop, Topanga." The announcer says over the speaker.

I work the knife around the edge of the locket's clasp. It still won't open. As the train starts to slow and begins braking, I try one more time. Suddenly, a violent burst of light fills the car. I feel like I'm floating and shooting down into the floor at the same time. Grabbing hold of Patches, she is stiff and her eyes are fixed. The light on her chest is off. The train shudders and stops. And then the whole train... disappears.

I am left standing in the middle of nowhere. Patches reboots and starts barking. Looking around, I can see that everything is familiar but completely changed. There are no digital signs. No buildings. No cars. Only earth and hills as far as I can see. Then off to the right, I see a small person standing not too far from me.

"You made it!" she exclaims. She seems unsurprised and very happy to see us. She's slight with long black hair. She walks over.

"I am Chumash. Do you speak Chumashan? Hokan? Spanish or English?"

I nod at English, and before Patches can google Chumashan and start translating, she starts talking again.

"My name is Lahui but you can call me Lu", she says. "We use nicknames instead of our given names. Much safer. Keeps people from having supernatural powers over us. What's your name?"

"I'm Pamm. With two M's", I say sheepishly. "But I don't have a nickname".

"Hi Pamm with two M's. I'm going to give you a nickname. Let's call you Speed since you travelled faster than the speed of light to get here. There! Now we both have nicknames so we won't alarm the tribal elders."

She laughs. And her laugh is so real it makes me laugh too. I like her immediately.

I introduce her to Patches and she introduces me to a small black and white spotted rat she carries in her pocket named Shunu. Patches, who hates rats, growls at Shunu. Then she whimpers and the two sniff each other nose to nose.

Lu tells us she was on her way to teach music to the town kids. "But it's not every day we get a visitor through the portal. I'm going to take you to meet Kanyon, the Dream Catcher. She will be so pleased!"

We start hiking up the trail to the top of the hill overlooking the valley. It is quite steep in places, with Manzanita bushes on either side and giant Engelmann Oaks dotting the landscape as far as the eye can see. Patches catalogues and announces the names of plants and insects we pass –Warbler, Beetle, Toxicodendron Diversilobum (Poison Oak).

We stop for a break in the shade and Lu asks, "Do you like games?" Followed by, "You must have lots of friends where you come from?" And later "what's the future like." I'm not sure how to answer so many questions. "Yes, I like games. No, I don't have many friends. The future is... all I know I guess."

Lu teaches me how to play Shinny and Hoop and Pole, but says she's only allowed to play Shinny because she's a girl. We agree that's totally unfair. I show her my wristband and play music which makes her laugh. Before you know it, Lu's playing her clapper stick and we are dancing around, singing our own made up words. Patches who is programmed to correct grammatical errors, gets overwhelmed and rolls over on her side.

"This is the most fun I can remember having." I say.

"Me too." Lu says. "But we should get going before it gets too late. They continue to climb up the hill.

When they reach the top, they find the dream catcher sitting on a stool where the sun shines brightest.

"I'm going to tell you two something" Kanyon says. "In the story of the Three Worlds, there is the world we currently live in, the world below us held up by two serpents, and the world above us, sustained by the great eagle. But this is only a story. The truth is, there is no space and time. Only this very moment. The Eternal Now. Infinite possibilities. But you must always be careful of dark matter. It lurks where their eyes cannot see."

She tells us that we must hurry up and go. She knows of only one tunnel back. Hidden in the rock formations outside of Sullivan's Pass.

"But I just got here. I'm not ready to go." I say.

I can't believe how good even the air smells, how beautiful the hills and the trees. This strange immediate connection I feel with Lu. Nobody back home makes me feel this way. Not even Sam or Mom. I look to Lu for support.

Lu, knowing her place and not wanting to upset the dream catcher, is careful with her words. "Today was so much fun. The most fun!"

The dream catcher continues... "You must go now. Go! Follow the path towards the ocean breeze. Stay on course. Don't look back. There are members of the tribe who won't understand. Lu's brother and his friends in the brotherhood of the canoe. Good men. Well meaning, but closed minds. Whatever you do, don't leave the path."

"You must walk 7,369 steps to Grand Arch. It is made up of rocks and minerals of many shapes. When the sun has shifted the the farthest corner of the west look to the ground. You will see in it's shadow the outline of a pentagram. Stand in the center of it, touch metal to your locket and the tunnel will open."

"Lu... DO NOT go through the tunnel. The locket is your friend's key to travel. You must have your own key or you will not be able to get back."

We leave and set off for Sullivan's Pass. Lu takes my hand and Patches, who is such a good dog, lets Shunu ride on her head. We move in a pack, swiftly and quietly. Others can be seen farther down the trail, but we stay to the inner edge and out of sight. As we reach the Grand Arch, the alarm on my wristband sounds.

SOMETHING BETTER BEGINNING

♡♡

PERSON: Charley Sunshine, female, 30-something bookseller

PLACE: New York City

THING: Mechanical Calliope

♡

I wouldn't say I fell in love at first sight with Charley Sunshine. It was something else. I was both put off and impressed by her at the same time. I walked into her bookshop looking for a decent used copy of *Confederacy of Dunces*. I was feeling especially lonely that day and didn't care too much whether the book was there or not. I really just needed some human contact.

"New York is cold, but I like where I'm living. There's music on Clinton Street all through the evening." I thought of the words to Leonard Cohen's Famous Blue Raincoat often. It was my anthem since moving to this city four months prior. Though technically the song was about a love triangle, I always thought of it as a lonely man's letter of lament. I was a cynical romantic. I moved to New York to escape California heartache... and also because my video production company relocated. It wasn't *my* company, per se, in the sense that Charley's bookstore was hers. But I'd been there eight years and was their primary shooter. We mostly did corporate videos and soul-sucking commercials, but I got paid well, and I felt like I was less of a sellout than if I sold insurance or the like.

My true passion was Super 8 filmmaking. I'd made a bunch of films with my West Coast friends as actors, and I also loved working with found footage. I was a John Cassavetes die hard fan, desperately seeking his own Gena Rowlands.

So, when I walked into that barely noticeable bookshop in Soho, and saw her -- with her dark schoolgirl braids and big-collared 70s floral mini dress over perfectly faded dungarees -- I caught my breath. She wore little makeup, and had an innocence about her, but the lines at her eyes put her in her mid-30s, in my estimation. She definitely had a maturity about her, despite the childlike getup. My ex-girlfriend -- and all subsequent dates since -- were in their 20s and "figuring out" who they were.

Not Charley Sunshine. She knew who she was, alright. She exuded confidence and an "I don't care what people think" attitude. She looked up and smiled as the little bell rang on the front door. I was just about to smile back when she said, "Down, Oliver" and I realized she was smiling at the grey cat perched just behind my head on a top shelf of musty books.

I smiled anyway. I was just that kind of guy.

"Hi. Do you have a copy of *Confederacy of Dunces*?"

"Good God. Who wants to know?"

A beat. I was not sure what that "Good God" implied and suddenly felt an insecurity I hadn't felt in twenty years -- since high school.

"Um. Oprah? Oprah Winfrey? I'm her personal shopper."

Charley Sunshine's smiling eyes betrayed her.

"I would think Oprah read on a Kindle."

"Yeah, she usually does, but she likes to support brick-and-mortar stores on occasion."

"Cool. Tell her "thanks" for the three bucks. It'll help me stay in business for sure."

"Three bucks? You have a copy for only four bucks? Sold!"

"Sorry -- you gotta look yourself. Fiction's over there. Alphabetical by author. You can have any Oprah books for free."

I chuckled and headed to the designated fiction section to start searching through the Ts. Not there. Then I checked out the Ks. John Kennedy Toole? I tried in vain to remember my rules of alphabetizing, but I realized they just didn't have it. That's the crapshoot with used bookstores, but now what should I pretend to want to buy instead?

I didn't want to leave.

I browsed the Art and Film books. Went back to the front counter, where Charley was looking through a Time Out from a stack in front of her. That's when I learned her perfect name. That's when I became enamored and shot down at the same time.

"Got any recommendations? Read any good books lately?" I asked in an unfamiliar voice. Why so nervous?

"For you? Or Oprah?"

"Ha. Me. I'm Henry, by the way."

"Hi. Charley. Charley Sunshine."

I stifled a guffaw and smiled. "Cool name. You make it up?"

"No."

"Wow. You lucked into a name quite befitting."

"Well, I altered it a bit from Charlene Shorstein. So there's that. Look... Henry. Do you want to be my wedding date tonight? But I'm not going to fuck you. Just so you know."

(Hence the "putting me off" part.)

I was more than a little taken aback and very lacking for the right words, but I was saved by the bell, as it were. In walked an older man -- mid-sixties -- with a box of books. He seemed a regular.

"Hey, Charley. Buying today?"

"Hi, Fred. Let's make it quick, I'm closing early for a gig."

"Nice. Nice. Calliope?"

"Yeah. A friend-of-a-friend's surprise wedding."

"Surprise wedding? In my day, they called that shotgun." Fred seemed proud of this offering.

"No. Nothing like that. They invited a bunch of friends, told them to dress up, that it was an important party so BE THERE or else, type of thing. Then, they'll make their vows and call it a 'wedding'. So, I'm lugging my calliope on the subway... but I might have recruited some help." She gestured in my direction with a wink, where I was leaning up against a nearby bookshelf, trying to remember what a calliope looked like... or even sounded like. Also wondering if my recruitment would amount to anything, what with her previous ominous prediction.

I moseyed to the back of the store, though I was curious about what Fred was selling. They chatted a bit, as she looked through his stash, and I found a well-worn book on birdwatching in New York.

When Fred's business was done, he left, and Charley moved to switch the "Open" sign to "Shut".

"Wanna go?"

"To a wedding? For people I don't know? With someone I don't know? With whom I will not be sleeping? But who needs me to drag her instrument down the street? Sounds positively intriguing. I HAD been planning to hole up in my apartment with a bottle of wine and this." I showed her my bird book selection. "I hear the cats are killing all the songbirds. How much, by the way?"

She grinned again. Whenever she did that, she looked like a five-year-old, attempting to charm her daddy. Won me over every time. "Free for you, my wedding date and roadie!"

Then, she said, "I'm assuming you have a sharp suit of sorts, based on how meticulous you look for a bookstore visit?"

I looked down at my cardigan, tailored pants, Clark desert boots. Not so bad, I figured. And she was right. I had an awesome blue sharkskin early 60s suit that did right by me. I thought Charley Sunshine would approve. "I have a suit, Miss Shorstein."

Yikes. At that, she threw me a look that told me to never use her given name again. The kind of look that was not very sunshiney at all. Almost made me want to use it again, but I really wanted to be with her. Really wanted to see this surprise wedding. Really wanted to hear her play this calliope.

"I'll be right back. C'mon, Oliver."

She waited for the grey kitty to navigate the piles of books and tables, and they ascended up a circular stairway in the back. I followed with my gaze, and it was only then I spotted the instrument in the far left back corner. It looked like an antique steam organ. Very decorative, and it fit right in with the vibe of the shop. The calliope! Beautiful, ornate, dated but in an elegant and appropriate way, like Charley, herself. It had pipe-like whistles at the top, a keyboard, a roll like the old player pianos in Farrell's ice cream shops.

My mind started swirling with excitement over the unexpected evening's events. What would happen? Would I meet new friends? Would she and I become inseparable? Would I become a calliope enthusiast? Could I bring my Super 8 with me?

Just then, she descended, in a little black sequined dress, her braids pinned to the top of her head, a bottle of Maker's Mark in her hand.

"Wanna hear something?" She flipped a switch, and the calliope started whistling. I was instantly transported to the old carousel I used to ride with my grandmother. It was playing "Beautiful

Dreamer", and I had the distinct feeling it was quite appropriate for this new friendship.

"I play more current stuff when I play it. Some originals. You'll hear!"

"I eagerly await..."

"I'll be right back. Need my shoes. Hold this." She handed me the whiskey, gave me another flash of her charming smile and went back upstairs.

"I eagerly await..."

As I stood there, listening to the music, searching in vain for something to put in my ears to soften the sounds of the thundering instrument, I heard her muffled voice, followed by a prolonged wail come from above -- a wailing so loud and sorrowful, I could still hear it over the calliope.

I wasn't entirely sure what to do. Wait for her to come down? See if she beckoned me up?

I waited. For what felt like hours but must have been... ten minutes, maybe? I waited through "Oh Susanna" and "When the Saints Come Marching In".

When I heard a loud thump on the ceiling above my head, I realized it was time to investigate. As I carefully crept up the creaking staircase, the calliope transitioned to "My Bonnie Lies over the Ocean", and I felt inexplicable tears welling up in my eyes.

Was this the start of another heartbreak... or was something better beginning? The Kinks were battling it out in my head with the calliope tune for theme song of the night.

I reached the top of the stairs and found her bedroom, a poetic vision just as I'd imagined, with a low bed and half-burned candles, a turntable, thrift store paintings, a vintage armoire. I didn't see Charley Sunshine at first, though.

Then, I saw her form on the floor by the head of the bed, a crumpled figure in black. Her cell phone lay on the bed, ringing from "Mom's Cell."

"Charley?" I said, my voice barely a whisper. I could still hear the booming instrument below. "Charley?" I repeated, so she could hear.

I instinctively went to hold her, and she let me.

"I've just lost the only man I've ever loved," she whispered, and it was in that moment that I achingly and fiercely yearned to be the second.

APPENDIX I: ASSIGNMENTS FROM GINNY

(AKA How We Did It)

Before beginning, invite someone into the creative process with you. See what happens. Go from there.

HALF & HALF

- Agree on a due date. One week is best.
- Each person writes half of a story.
- Do not share anything about your story with each other.
- When you are done with your half of a story, send it to the other person.
- Read the other person's half of a story ONLY upon finishing and sending them your own.
- Take another week to finish the story you've been given.
- Now swap and send the now completed stories to each other.

SAME START/FINISH

- One person chooses a random starting sentence.
- The other person chooses a random ending sentence.
- Set a due date. One week is best.
- Both people write a story - each using the same starting and ending sentence.

PERSON, PLACE & THINGS

- Each person chooses a Person, a Place and a Thing.
- Send it to the other person. These are the elements they must include in their story.
- Agree on a due date. 2 weeks is best.
- Write a story using the "prompts" the other person has supplied.
- Finish and share!

APPENDIX II: THE THREE C'S

(AKA What Happened to Stefanie)

Lastly, I feel compelled to share some health details that are completely irrelevant to this book, but if it educates one person or changes the course of anyone's experience, then it will be worth it.

Stefanie was diagnosed with Crohn's in her twenties, a chronic inflammatory bowel disease managed with medications. What she did not know, was that people with Crohn's (as well as people with Colitis, another inflammatory bowel disease) are more prone to develop Colon Cancer or Cholangeocarcinoma (Bile Duct Cancer).

Stefanie ended up with both, one right after the other. Colon Cancer in 2017 which she successfully fought off. Then Cholangeocarcinoma (Bile Duct Cancer) in 2019.

If we were writing a story, Stefanie might choose "bad break" or "dealt two terrible hands in a row" to describe this news. In any event, if you take some time to google, you'll quickly realize the serious nature of her diagnosis. And how rare it is. Although, not really as rare as it first had seemed.

To the surgeons, doctors and medical staff at Kaiser Oakland, thank you for your efforts and care. The women who delivered and managed Stefanie's chemo (another C!) treatments were, and are, heroic and kind. Exuberant and earnest at the same time. I'd be remiss to not shout out specifically to Shoshana, who was a constant through both bouts of Stefanie's cancer treatments. More than a care provider, Stefanie once said Shoshana was "a lot like us". Meaning, I think, someone we would hang out with even if cancer weren't involved.

My spouse Ginny, our writing taskmaster, was an unflinching resource and support for Stefanie. The voice of calm reason and researched knowledge who Stefanie could call and run her thoughts and emotions by first. Ginny was also an ardent and incredible supporter of me, as was my friend Beth, who reminded me to always show up with an open heart.

Last but not least, to our dear sister, Stacy. Thank you so much for the very first writing assignment. Thank you for always being a great sister and for being Stefanie's twin. And a lifetime of thanks for caring for Stefanie during her hospice, alongside our mom Sandy, and helping Stefanie make her way to the other side.

I love you. Let me know if you want to write something together.

APPENDIX III: PUSS IN: BOOTY CALL

(AKA a Short Play Adapted from the Short Story "Loneliness")

SETTING:

Monday night dinner time inside a small apartment. Within the one room there is a small kitchen-type table with two chairs, a loveseat size couch and a door to the bedroom. The stage is split with a half-wall to separate the living room from the bathroom. LOLA sits at the small kitchen table by herself. CARMINE sits on a stool near the counter. At rise: *LOLA, a 30-something single woman, dressed in black yoga pants and a sweatshirt, and CARMINE, her roommate/cat dressed in all black. Two live musicians provide music.*

CARMINE *(to audience)*: It's just a chicken pot pie. The same she's eaten every Monday night for as long as I can remember.

(*LOLA begins to cry as she eats her pot pie. We hear The Big Bang Theory on TV. She begins to wail louder, as something has snapped in her. There is a pounding on the wall, a neighbor. She bangs back on the wall. She picks up her cell phone and looks over at CARMINE.)*

CARMINE: Don't... Don't do it.

(*LOLA texts something reluctantly. Does not hit "send".)*

CARMINE: Did you just text him? Did you? What did you write? Did you write 'Come over."? Tell me you didn't write 'come over'.

LOLA: I didn't write 'come over'.

(*CARMINE starts to approach, to read what she wrote.)*

LOLA: Fine. I wrote it. But I didn't hit "send".

CARMINE: I'm just looking out for you, Kiddo.

(*LOLA starts to cry again. She picks up the phone, looks at CARMINE. Hits "send.")*

CARMINE: Dammit, Lola. That was a mistake.

LOLA: No, what's a mistake is that I didn't pick up nail polish remover at Walgreen's earlier. Shit. Shit. Shit.

(LOLA grabs purple nail polish and tries to "touch up" her toenails.)

CARMINE: He doesn't care about your chipped *toenail* polish. They never do.

LOLA: I care.

CARMINE: Are you gonna change out of your Inside-Outs?

LOLA: Inside-Outs are the yoga pants that can be worn anywhere.

CARMINE: In theory.

(CARMINE rolls his eyes. LOLA goes over to her bedroom area and slips off her stretch pants. She looks for something else to wear.)

LOLA *(looks over her shoulder towards the living room):* I'm changing. Maybe something that looks accidentally sexy?

CARMINE: Tight jeans?

LOLA: YES! These?

(She puts on her tight jeans and we can tell she's having a memory as she fights back tears.)

LOLA: These are the ones he commented on that time in the cafe. Remember, I told you about that time?

CARMINE: I have a vague recollection of you telling me about that time. A few times.

(LOLA puts on a form-fitting "ringer" band i.e. "Wilco" T-shirt.)

CARMINE: A well-known winner with the lads.

(LOLA goes to the living room sofa and checks her phone. Relief washes over her face as she realizes he's returned her text.)

LOLA: Carmine, listen. He writes: "I thought you didn't want to do this anymore?" Winky emoji.

CARMINE: Yeah! I thought you DIDN'T want to do it anymore?

(CARMINE gets up and stretches, catlike, before returning to same position as before.)

LOLA *(saying and texting at the same time):* "I don't."

(She hits "send")

LOLA: Oh wait. I don't want him to get the wrong idea. "But isn't that what makes it so... enticing? Winky emoji". Better.

(LOLA *is sort of smitten with her own wittiness and smiles to herself. CARMINE rolls his eyes and goes over to lay across the bed. The TV starts playing music and we hear the announcement of a new show starting: Law & Order: SVU.)*

(CARMINE gets up and moves back to curl up on the living room couch.)

CARMINE *(to audience):* This is an addiction. *(To LOLA)* Lola, do you want to turn this off? For your date?

LOLA: It's not a date.

(CARMINE waits... anticipates)

LOLA: We're hanging out.

CARMINE: I see. "Spending time?"

LOLA: Yeah. Exactly.

(LOLA finishes and gets up to put something away in the medicine cabinet. As she shuts the cabinet, she catches her reflection in the mirror and begins to sob again.)

(CARMINE tiptoes to the bathroom to check on her. He walks up behind her and puts his hands (paws) on her shoulders.)

(LOLA *relaxes under his touch and takes a deep breath. She perks up and heads out of the bathroom, followed by CARMINE. She notices this, picks up a cat toy, tosses it back into the bathroom.)*

LOLA: In you go, Carmine. Good boy.

(LOLA also drags in a cat litter box. CARMINE *walks thru the bathroom doorway. This is the first time it's obvious he's a cat. CARMINE thinks she's going to follow him in but LOLA quickly closes the door behind her. CARMINE is shocked - not because he's surprised but because he can't believe he fell for it again.)*

CARMINE *(to audience)*: Fell for it again.

(LOLA tidies the apartment and turns off the TV.)

CARMINE: I'm so goddamn tired of her shenanigans.

(The door intercom buzzes. LOLA goes over to ring 'HIM' up. She moves a few things back to how they were to make her apartment look a tad messier. Then she assumes a nonchalant pose on the couch, with the NYT crossword. Soon there is a knock on the front door.)

LOLA: Coming!

(The light in the living room goes dark and the light and action shifts to CARMINE in the bathroom. He hears her open the front door and splays out flat on the floor peaking under the crack at the bottom of the door. He then gets up, goes around the bathroom door to the front of the stage.)

CARMINE *(to audience):* At this point, we'd like to ask for a volunteer from the audience. Preferably male-identifying. Beyond that, anyone will do. It doesn't matter. It never really matters who the guy is.

CARMINE *(to audience volunteer):* Thank you, Sir. May I ask your name? And what do you do?

CARMINE (*to audience, improvising):* Can we give a round of applause to ____ the _____. (i.e. Scott the Dentist). *(After applause)* But it doesn't really matter what his name is or what he does. Or that he's... just not that into her. Because she... she will love him.

(CARMINE will throw an army jacket on the audience member. He escorts him over to the dark stage and puts him next to LOLA, who in turn takes the audience member's hand.)

(CARMINE retreats back to bathroom. No longer emcee, now cat again. As much to himself as to anyone he begins to talk...)

CARMINE: Imitation Army Jacket? What a poser! She picks the winners. And are those Diesel jeans? Ach! Typical. They're always a financial consultant or ____ *(audience member's real profession i.e. dentist)* by day.

(Beat)

"Lothario by night" *(sarcastically).*

(Beat)

Unshaven. Clearly she likes her men hairy. *(Or whatever improv will work with volunteer. If clean cut, "clean cut. I thought she liked her men hairy" etc.)*

LOLA *(in a sexy voice):* I'm glad you came. I know I said I didn't want to talk about other people we see, but, just so you know, things didn't work out with that Pete guy.

CARMINE *(to audience):* "Things didn't work out" because she didn't let things work out. That Pete guy was PERFECT for her. Well, not as perfect as someone else around here, but still...

(CARMINE gets up and looks at himself in the mirror. Admires himself from all sides.)

LOLA: I mean, he just... didn't do it for me... the way you do.

(LOLA starts flirtatious talking as she guides volunteer towards bedroom.)

CARMINE *(to audience):* Because Pete was decent, respectful and an animal-lover. Not a booty-caller.

(Bedroom door closes. This gets CARMINE's *attention.)*

CARMINE *(louder and in her direction):* Yeah, Pete showed interest in you and your life. He was a nice guy. You liked the same things!

(MUSICIANS start playing Marvin Gaye's Sexual Healing or similar slow sexy song.)

CARMINE: I don't know how much more a cat can take.

I'm on my ninth life with this one.

Alexa, play Carmine's playlist.

(Marvin Gaye turns off. MUSICIANS *start to play hip hop/jazz style and CARMINE starts dancing. As he goes thru his routine he is oblivious to the fact he is creating chaos all around him - knocking the soap dish off the sink, crashing into the shelves, knocking over the trash can. He hops down off of the toilet and pull the chenille bath mat off the "tub"(or rack) for good measure. He strides back and forth across the bath mat to the beat of the music, then stops and pulls out a few tufts of cotton. It feels good and he relishes in his accomplishment - almost ecstatic - but then the moment passes and he's feeling surly again.*

The song changes to something slower and CARMINE finishes his dance and takes a big bow. Then curls up on top of the pile of towels and falls asleep.

A few beats pass and we hear an occasional laugh or movement from off-stage/bedroom. The stage is still dark except for a nightlight in the bathroom. CARMINE is *still fast asleep.*

LOLA quietly creeps towards the bathroom door barefoot in her silk bathrobe. She starts to open the door but hits resistance as CARMINE is sleeping too close to it and it can't be full opened. She's not sure what the impediment is, but tries to slip thru the crack she's made. In the process, she accidentally steps on his foot.)

CARMINE: AHHHH!!! HEY!!!!!

LOLA: Shhhh... it's okay. It's just me. It's okay. Shhhhhh.

CARMINE: What?!? You stepped on me.

LOLA: Oops, sorry. I have to pee. *(She giggles and shrugs).*

(LOLA passes him and sits down on the toilet. Finishes and then starts to get up to leave.)

CARMINE: We need to talk.

LOLA: Like, now?

(*CARMINE nods his head.)*

(LOLA puts the toilet lid back down and takes a seat. CARMINE squats down in front of her.)

CARMINE (*Takes a deep audible breath.)*: You need to treat me better.

LOLA: I love you Carmine honey. But can we talk tomorrow?

CARMINE: *(sad, earnest)*: I may not be here tomorrow.

LOLA: Don't be silly. Of course you will.

CARMINE: No. Maybe I won't. You take me for granted. You lock me in the bathroom. I do everything for you and you treat me like a...

LOLA *(getting up)*: Would you feel safer in your travel kennel? Or we could build you a fortress in one of the kitchen cabinets? *(She motions towards the kitchen.)*

CARMINE: Cat.

LOLA: Honey, you are a cat. *(She reaches over to pet his head. He bats her hand away.)*

CARMINE: I am more than this fur and bones!

LOLA: Okay. Let's continue this in the morning. Alright? What's-his-name's still here.

CARMINE: I watch you night after night, crying in your Whole Foods pot pie, watching your SVU reruns!

LOLA: I thought you liked SVU?

CARMINE: I don't. I do it to be with you.

LOLA: Oh.

CARMINE: You're blind to the possibilities.

LOLA: This really isn't like you. Where's that positive cat-itude

CARMINE: We're stuck in a rut and there's nothing I can do.

LOLA: Really. I don't understand. And you know, he's waiting.

CARMINE: Yeah. "He's" waiting. Go ahead. Run away. Go! Go!

LOLA *(with hand on doorknob):* I wouldn't but...

CARMINE: What happened to Pete?

LOLA: Pete? He didn't even like me.

CARMINE: Why? Because he wouldn't sleep with you on the first date?

LOLA: Or second or third.

CARMINE: He told you he wanted to wait!

LOLA: Forget about Pete.

CARMINE: I won't. He liked me. And he liked you! I could tell.

LOLA: That's done. Now I have what's-his-name.

CARMINE: Who'll be gone again before breakfast.

LOLA: Pete was too hard to read. I think he was gay.

CARMINE: Why? Because he liked you and wanted to know you better? And isn't a player.

LOLA: Maybe.

CARMINE: Real relationships are hard. And he's not gay.

LOLA: How do you know?

CARMINE: I'm Gay. And I've got pretty good gaydar.

LOLA: You're not gay.

CARMINE: I am. But that's another play.

LOLA: Huh, how did I not know?

CARMINE: And another thing. What's-his-name… what was this one's name?

(*LOLA & CARMINE improvise here about the audience member's name, profession, etc.)*

LOLA: Scott.

CARMINE: Oh yeah. Scott. Scott the dentist.

LOLA: Yeah.

CARMINE: He is a LOSER. He makes you feel like shit.

LOLA: I know. I've got to get rid of him.

CARMINE: One more time: you don't even know the guy. Might as well have wandered in off the street…

(to audience) Or from the audience.

LOLA *(backing out the door):* I love you, Carm.

(LOLA starts making kissing noises and little waves at him. CARMINE sits down on the floor by the toilet, dejected, head in hands.)

LOLA: Sorry, have to close this door. Okay. Bye bye.

(She closes door and sneaks back to the bedroom. CARMINE falls asleep. In the dark, the front door opens and closes. Audience Member leaves without fanfare.

Stage lights dim and then brighten, signaling day break. LOLA emerges from bedroom, opens bathroom door. She appears happy. She is humming. Picks up CARMINE's hands and does a quick little dance with him. Then she heads to kitchen and starts preparing breakfast. Pouring cereal in a bowl, putting things out on the table etc.)

CARMINE (*to audience):* I don't get it. She's usually depressed the morning after.

LOLA: I heard that.

CARMINE: *I'm* usually depressed the morning after.

LOLA: Yep, heard that too.

(LOLA has a thought and looks for her phone. She finds her phone. Begins to call someone.)

CARMINE: Who are you calling? You never do this...

LOLA: Hi, Pete? It's me, Lola. So... sorry I never got back to you. I was... figuring stuff out. Are you still... free?

(LOLA and CARMINE share a look.)

LOLA: Really? How sweet. I've been thinking about you, too. Yeah, we... DID... have a good time...

(CARMINE rubs up against her, affectionately, as she talks.)

CARMINE *(comes forward, speaks to audience):* Think I should feel threatened? Jealous of this cat, Pete? No way. She didn't lock me in the bathroom for him.

LOLA *(interjecting, still on phone):* I'd never have to lock you in the bathroom, if you didn't do your "staring thing".

CARMINE: All cats stare.

LOLA: Well, it's creepy when you're trying to...you know...get down.

CARMINE: I'll stop staring if Pete's around.

LOLA *(back on phone call):* Sorry. I'm here. My cat was needing some attention.

CARMINE: I'll always need attention. Some lovey-dovey talk. A few scratches under my chin. If I have that, I won't mind if she has someone else to share breakfast with.

(CARMINE does one last jig/dance -- with her, still on phone).

... as long as I still get to lick the cereal bowl when she's through.

www.ingramcontent.com/pod-product-compliance
Lightning Source LLC
Chambersburg PA
CBHW061126100726
47911CB00013B/699

* 9 7 8 0 5 7 8 7 7 6 6 0 6 *